How to
Take a Chance

How to Take a Chance

By DARRELL HUFF

Illustrated by IRVING GEIS

W · W · NORTON & COMPANY · INC · New York

FOR LAURIE AND KRISTY,

WHO ARE BEGINNING TO SHOW AN INTEREST

ISBN 0 393 05281 8 Cloth Edition
ISBN 0 393 00263 2 Paper Edition

Library of Congress Catalog Card No. 58-13953

PRINTED IN THE UNITED STATES OF AMERICA

0

Contents

All Nature is but Art, unknown to thee;
All Chance, Direction, which thou canst not see . . .

—Alexander Pope

He who has heard the same thing told by 12,000 eye-witnesses
has only 12,000 probabilities, which are equal to one strong
probability, which is far from certainty.

—Voltaire

A reasonable probability is the only certainty.

—E. W. Howe

It is truth very certain that, when it is not in our power to
determine what is true, we ought to follow what is most probable.

—René Descartes

If you had it all to do over, would you change anything? "Yes,
I wish I had played the black instead of the red at Cannes and
Monte Carlo."

—Winston Churchill

This branch of mathematics [probability] is the only one, I
believe, in which good writers frequently get results entirely
erroneous.

—Charles Sanders Peirce

HOUSE RUNS INTO CAR

Home Being Moved Dents Fender of Automobile

HAMPTON, S.C. (AP)—Mrs. Eloise Goreau had an unlikely explanation when her husband asked how one fender of their car became dented.

"A house ran into it," she said.

It was true. A house mover was moving a small house down a street and a corner of the house hit the car, parked in front of the Goreau home.

'GO' SIGNAL OFTEN FATAL

R. I. Auto Club Cites 10% Killed Crossing With Light

PROVIDENCE, R. I. (UPI) —You apparently stand a better chance of getting killed in Rhode Island by crossing intersections with the traffic light than against it.

According to the Automobile Club of Rhode Island, "10 per cent of all pedestrians killed at intersections in 1957 were crossing with the signal, while 6 per cent were crossing against it."

"These figures prove conclusively that it is dangerous to assume that the 'go' signal on the traffic light relieves the pedestrian of the need for alertness," it adds.

British Hunter Is Shot By a Fox in Its Burrow

TREGONY, England, May 29 (Reuters)—The Foxes of old England are wily creatures—and Mike Sara of this Cornish hamlet has wounds to prove it.

Mr. Sara, 20 years old, spotted a cub on an outing yesterday, wounded it with a blast from his double-barreled shotgun and chased the crippled fox as it fled into its burrow. He poked the butt of his gun down the hole, the second barrel fired and he fell down wounded.

Farmers who found him pulled the shotgun out of the hole. The fox cub, dead of its wounds, came with it—one paw hooked around the trigger.

Man Pays Parking Tax, Gets $96,000 in Change

H. I. Hamiton of Queensland, wanted to pay his parking tax but had only a note of large denomination which the authorities couldn't change.

According to News Mail of Adelaide, Australia, he accepted a lottery ticket in lieu of change and it just won the first prize. Hamilton is now $96,000 richer.

Introduction

IF YOU GO fox-hunting will you shoot a fox? Will a fox shoot you?

Could life on earth have begun spontaneously?

How many of an item must a storekeeper stock to be reasonably certain he won't run out?

How far can you trust an opinion poll?

When is insurance a good buy?

What does "probable" mean?

How likely is it that the eventual winner in an election will be ahead all the way?

What's the doctrine of the maturity of chances? Why is it so costly?

Why is the sky blue? When will this book fly into the air?

How is a long-range weather forecast made?

What hope have parents of five daughters for a change next time around?

How far has the existence of telepathy been demonstrated?

When is a medical miracle not a miracle?

Where is the fatal weakness in every gambling system?

Just what does the law of averages really say?

These are a few of the mass of questions with which the theories of probability deal. This tiny list barely touches on the whole field of probability because probability touches on almost everything.

"Life is a school of probability," said Walter Bagehot, and it is indeed. In flouting, or failing to grasp, the laws of chance we hurt ourselves in many ways. We buy insurance we don't need and we fail to insure the risks we should. We make damaging decisions in business and in driving a car. We flip from overpessimism to unguided optimism and back. We invest in systems at roulette, play unnecessarily bad bridge, and draw to inside straights.

We produce all sorts of reasonable but entirely false bits of logic, blithely crediting them to the laws of chance. We introduce many of our most splendid, and most damaging, pieces of superstition with the ringing words, "The Law of Averages says . . . " In doing so we create in ourselves and in our affairs a kind of accident-proneness.

Most serious of all, we neglect an acute tool for understanding our world. Physics, nuclear and other, is coming more and more to talk in the language of chance. Research in medicine and the social sciences can often be understood only through statistical methods that have grown out of probability theory. Today's politics, tomorrow's weather, and next week's satellite—all call for judgment and action through a recognition of probabilities and what they mean.

It is with the truth and the nonsense in things as large and as small as these that this book deals.

How to
Take a Chance

CHAPTER 1

Girl or Boy, Heads or Tails?

How to figure the even chances, and why d'Alembert went wrong.

OUR FRIENDS the Mortons have two daughters. Like a good many other people they regard two boys and two girls as the ideal family.

"After the girls were born," Bob remarked the other night, "we began to doubt that we'd come out two and two in the end. But I have it figured now: our chances were fifty-fifty in the beginning, so of course they still are. Because boys are just as likely as girls."

Bob's situation rather neatly illustrates a basic problem in the probability of even chances. It has equivalents in tossing coins for heads or tails or in playing any of the even chances on a roulette wheel. By extension his problem applies to all sorts of more serious situations, from safely shielding an atomic reactor to marketing a new electric iron.

But is Bob's solution correct?

Let's begin by testing the notion that a newly married couple planning to issue two children has an even chance of getting one boy and one girl, in either order.

Assuming for the moment that boys and girls are born with equal frequency (which is close enough to the truth for our purpose), each child is as likely to be a boy as a girl.

The two children then may be boy and girl, or two boys, or two girls. Three possibilities. All equally likely? No.

What we really have is four equal possibilities masquerading as three. They are: boy-boy, girl-girl, boy-girl, girl-boy. So, in fact, two of the four possibilities consist of a boy and a girl. There is indeed an even chance of a mixed pair in two children.

But what of the Mortons' optimistically planned four? In that number there are not four possibilities but sixteen. In listing them we'll take care to list them all and not fall again into the trap of regarding two or more of the possibilities as a single one even though, from the Mortons' point of view, order of arrival is not included among the specifications.

The sixteen possible sequences are: BBBB, BBBG, BBGB, *BBGG*, BGBB, *BGBG*, *BGGB*, BGGG, GBBB, *GBBG*, *GBGB*, GBGG, *GGBB*, GGBG, GGGB, GGGG.

Six of these, indicated by italics, give the desired mix of two boys and two girls. So the Mortons should have figured when they started reproducing that their chances

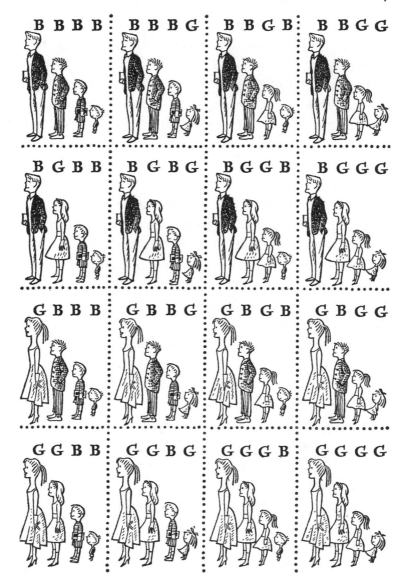

of coming out with two boys and two girls, in any order, were six in sixteen, or three in eight. Not quite so good as Bob guessed.

The charting of possibilities makes some other things evident. One is that there are two chances in sixteen (or one in eight) that your four children will be all of the same sex. And one chance in sixteen that all will be of either one or the other specified sex.

As father of four, all daughters, I am prepared to testify that this fairly long chance of one in sixteen does in fact occur, and of course this is something we have all observed.

Whether runs of this kind actually occur more often than once in sixteen times is an interesting question, which unfortunately has not yet found an answer. If patterns of sex distributions in families really are random, then the parents of four girls—or a dozen—can still properly feel that they have an even chance of a boy next time for a change.

But perhaps there is a factor to disturb this, something that makes boys run in a family. As Clarence P. Oliver, University of Texas geneticist, suggested to me recently, "It seems that some few individuals carry determiners which affect the X or Y sperms in fertilization."

And Amram Scheinfeld, who has done some excellent writing on heredity, cites investigations at Oxford University indicating that families with six or more sons and no daughters occur twice as often as chance says they should.

He adds that: "The odds against the occurrence of such

record all-son families as the Grover C. Joneses (Peterson, West Virginia) with fifteen sons, and the Emory Harrisons (Johnson City, Tennessee), with thirteen sons, are so astronomically high that pure chance as a causative factor is virtually ruled out."

Now it might be interesting to know just how astronomical the odds really are in a case like one of these. It will also give us a chance to tackle the method of figuring such an improbable probability.

One way to look at it is this. With a family of one child there are two possibilities: boy or girl. With two children there are the four possibilities listed earlier. Make a similar tabulation for three children and you'll find eight possibilities.

For four children there are the sixteen sequences listed for the Mortons earlier in this chapter.

It is beginning to be clear that the number of possible arrangements—called "permutations"—can be found by multiplying together as many 2's as there are children in the family. In the instance of four children the sequences total $2 \times 2 \times 2 \times 2$, or 2^4, or 16.

This brings us back to the thirteen sons of the Harrisons of Tennessee. Since 2^{13} (2 multiplied by itself 12 times) works out to 8,192 we know that these youngsters might have been arranged in any of that number of ways.

It is evident that only two of the arrangements would consist solely of one sex—that is, the one that is boy-boy-boy, etc., and the one that is girl-girl-girl. This is true no matter what the number of children.

So the chance of a family like the Harrisons' is 2 in 8,192 or 1 in 4,096. Another way of saying this is that we might expect one all-same-sex sequence for every four-thousand-odd families of this size. And if the population does contain some thousands of large families, as of course it does, something like the Harrisons' run of luck is to be expected.

It may very well be that more than chance is involved in producing some one-sided families,* but this case fails

One chance out of 136,657,480,245,248

* In more than a century, seven generations of the Pitofsky family have produced only sons. In 1959 the forty-seventh consecutive boy in the line was born to Mr. and Mrs. Jerome Pitofsky of Scarsdale, N.Y., or so the *New York Times* reported. Assuming no overlooked girls and no

to prove it.

Like boys and girls, heads and tails in coin-tossing offer an instance of equal probabilities. (So do certain wagers on a roulette wheel—the bets on red or black or even or odd or the first or the second half of the numbers. The roulette case is complicated, however, by the fact that the odds are not *quite* even, so let's stick to coin-tossing for a while and go into roulette later.)

To find the probability of any sequence or occurrence in coin-tossing or other equal-odds situation, you need only list all the possibilities and then count up the ones that meet your requirement.

Making the list is simple enough if you tackle it systematically. Using H and T to stand for heads and tails, the two possible results of one toss become H and T. For two tosses, add successively an H and a T to each of the first two. This will give you HH, TH, HT, TT. For a sequence of three tosses, add successively H and T to each of those four. And so on.

The picture on the next page shows how you can easily do this by making one column after another of alternating H's and T's, doubling the number each time. Connect as shown, and read by starting with the first column and following the connecting links across until you have used each letter in the last column to end a sequence.

---

distortions of the record in the interests of a marvel, this is a one-chance-in-136-trillion occurrence. While pondering its significance, you may also want to consider this: the pattern of the last forty-seven births in your family is also one that would occur just once in 136 trillion times . . . on the average.

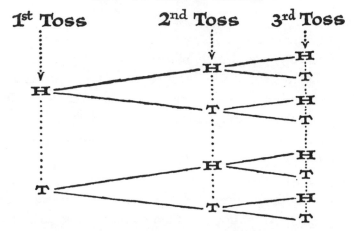

For some calculations, such as the likelihood of children (or heads and tails in coin-tossing) coming out fifty-fifty or in some other specific ratio, there is no really simple alternative to listing in this manner. But there is a method you'll find vastly quicker whenever the numbers involved become at all large. It's using Pascal's triangle, as shown in the solution to the last puzzle at the end of this book.

For other things you can apply rules, as we did for the Harrison family.

One rule: To find the probability of getting all of several different things, multiply together the chances of getting each one.

This applies to bearing boys, playing the red at roulette, and flipping nickels, as well as many other things.

What, for instance, is the likelihood of tossing heads any given number of times in a row? For one toss we've noted that the chance is one-half. For two tosses it is one-half times one-half, or one-fourth. For ten tosses it is the product of one-half taken ten times, which is about .00098, or a little less than one chance in a thousand.

From this it follows that if you want all of quite a few things and each of them is only fairly likely, your chance of getting them all is slight.

A way of looking at the likelihood of any occurrence is on a scale of zero to one. Zero represents no chance at all, an impossibility. One represents a sure thing. Fractions, all lying between zero and one, indicate probabilities. Thus the one-chance-in-two of a child's being a girl is indicated by one-half. The one-in-four that two children will both be girls is one-fourth.

All the possibilities in any case must add up to one. Of four children, the chances of two boys are one-fourth, of two girls one-fourth, of boy-and-girl one-half. These add up to one, which is to say a certainty that the result will be one of these three.

Most difficulties with probability lie in three areas: inequality of chances; small numbers of cases; and letting history creep in.

There is a story of a man torn between the duty of catching the 5:20 for home and the desire to stick around for another drink. He decided it would be proper to leave the decision up to chance. Flipping a dime he said, "Heads I'll have a straight shot, tails I'll have it with soda; and if the coin lands on edge I'll go home."

In making sure that the possibilities are equal it is well to begin by testing the assumptions. The dice must really be evenly balanced. The coin must have a head on one side only. The slot machine must not have been "fixed" to reduce the chances of its stopping in a payoff position. There must be no telekinesis operating (see Chapter 9) and there must be no cheating.

(Lord Hertford was once asked, "What would you do if you saw someone cheating at cards?" "What would I do?" he replied. "Bet on him, to be sure.")

For a sharp warning about the deceptive way unequal chances can creep in unnoticed, consider what might happen to you if you should accept the reasoning of the eminent eighteenth-century mathematician d'Alembert.

Let's say that your neighbor Joe is helping you kill a warm August evening and a couple of cans of beer.

"Let's toss coins," Joe proposes. "I'll toss first each time, then you. If either coin comes up heads I win. If neither, you win."

"That's okay," you answer cannily. "But there are three possibilities in a case like this, so d'Alembert says. You may get heads first and end the game right there. Or you may get tails and I get heads. Or we may both toss tails. In two of the three possible cases you win."

"Right," says Joe. "I have two chances to your one, so I'll put up $2 against $1."

Now the question is, is this a fair bet? D'Alembert said yes. If it isn't, where did d'Alembert—who made a number

JOE wins   *BUT if JOE fails to win on the first toss*

....he still has half a chance to win   *...and so do you*

of valuable contributions to mathematics—go wrong? And who will lose in the long run, you or Joe—and how much? And how might the odds be adjusted to turn this bet into a fair one?

The fallacy lies in the fact that the three possibilities named are not equal chances. One of them is actually twice as likely as either of the others. There is one chance in two that Joe will toss heads. There is one in four that he will toss tails and you will toss heads. Either way he wins, with a total probability of one-half plus one-fourth. The bet is three to one in his favor, and he should put up not $2 but $3 against your $1.

How much would you lose over a period of time in betting the way Joe and d'Alembert have encouraged you to? On the average, out of each four tosses you will win once and take in $2 and lose three times and pay out $3. Your net loss then will be $1 for each four games, or 25 cents for each, a pretty poor arrangement.

Please observe the words "period of time" and "on the average" in the paragraph above. Both phrases are there to act as warning signs. They are reminders that predictions of this sort are based on the law of large numbers. That is, you can not be reasonably sure that the prediction will be reasonably accurate if the number of trials or instances is small. But when it becomes large, the accuracy with which you can predict and the reliance you can place on your predictions increase.

Thus we know that while an honest coin tends to come heads half the time, on two or three or four tosses there is quite a good chance that it will fall tails every time. Increase the sequence to ten and it is unlikely that you'll get even 90% tails. Increase it to 100 or 1,000 and you can be almost sure that the ratio will be quite close to fifty-fifty.

It is important to distinguish between percentages and absolute numbers in this respect. The chance of getting exactly 50% heads (that is, precisely 2 out of 4 or 19 out of 38) is greater with a small number of tosses. But the chance of getting *approximately* 50% (say, between 45% and 55%) keeps on improving as the number of tosses is increased.

The number of cases, or size of sample, is fundamental to all sorts of applications of probability theory, and we shall come back to it frequently.

This brings us to the influence of history on chances, the most lively source of errors and confusion of all. The argument takes many forms:

"I've been holding terrible cards all evening. By the law of averages I should get very good hands from now on."

"It has rained nearly every day during the first half of May. Since on the average only half the days in May are wet in this climate, we can expect dry weather the rest of the month."

"We've had four girls in a row. Since the chances are 31 to one against five successive girls, we can practically count on a boy if we try again."

"I've kept a record on this roulette wheel for a month, and it has come up red 123 times more than black. Since by the law of averages red and black show up equally often, I can now clean up by betting on the black."

The fallacy—known as "the maturity of the chances"— is the same in every case. Things like cards and roulette wheels have no memories. Their future behavior is not affected by what has occurred in the past. The probability still remains fifty-fifty in each instance, but that is the probability for the future now, not for the total run including the one-sided past.

On August 18, 1913, at the Casino in Monte Carlo, black came up a record twenty-six times in succession. Except for the question of house limit, if a player had made a one-louis ($4) bet when the run started and pyramided for precisely the length of the run on black, he could have taken away 268 million dollars. What actually happened was a near-panicky rush to bet on red, beginning about the time black had come up a phenomenal fifteen times. In application of the maturity doctrine, players doubled and tripled their stakes, this doctrine leading them to believe after black came up the twentieth time that there was not a chance in a million of another repeat. In the end the unusual run enriched the Casino by some millions of francs.

The most likely expectation for the card player is average hands, just as it was when he started the evening and just as it will be when he sits down next time or a year from last Tuesday.

The total outlook for May is rainy, since we have a known wet spell to which to add a normal expectation for the rest of the month. On the average we can expect to end this May with a record of about three rainy days out of every four instead of the usual one in two.

The hopeful father has just the usual chance, roughly one in two, of a boy to break his string.

The roulette wheel, placidly forgetting that it has shown red disproportionately in the past, will tend to produce the two colors equally in the future. The best prediction of what our record-keeper will find when he totes up his books is about 123 more cases of red than of black.

The villain in all these instances is a frequently expensive error. It is the attempt to apply to the total of a series, part of which has been completed, the rule that fits only the unknown future.

This doctrine, however misguided, is an attempt to control chance. That's what the next chapter is about.

CHAPTER 2

How to Control Chance

*Planning your insurance,
backing roulette systems,
and replacing authors with apes.*

PEOPLE HAVE been trying for a long time to control risk, mainly by supplication, sacrifices, and hanging around oracles. These efforts add up to an enormous record of human superstition.

Playing a hunch, backing a lucky number, reading predictive value into a coincidence or a dream—each is an attempt to defeat chance. So is reliance on the fallacy of the maturity of the chances.

Yet there are intelligent approaches. One is Chauncey Depew's: "I am not at all superstitious, but I would not sleep thirteen in a bed on a Friday night."

More to the point is applying an understanding of odds

and a calculation of risks to the many hazards that are inevitable in life. This procedure will require you first to obtain facts about the probabilities of the situation. Then you must calculate something called the mathematical expectation. On top of that you must decide what risks, in light of your capital situation, you can afford.

Instead of floating around among generalities, let's pin this technique down to the day when you next buy or renew your automobile insurance. You might even save some money, at least the price of this book.

IT'S IN VERY GOOD CONDITION—I GOT IT FROM A LITTLE OLD LADY WHO ONLY DROVE TO CHURCH.

Begin with the most expensive part, personal liability. As a cautious driver of a well-kept car on which you put fewer miles each year than most people cover, you can be sure that your expectation is less than the cost of the policy.

Expectation is a concept that you will frequently find use for. It is the amount you will win in any gamble—such as insurance, speculation, or roulette—multiplied by the chances of your winning. If the odds of the game or gamble are set fairly, your expectation will be exactly equal to your stake; and you will break even in the long run. This is the situation in an amateur poker game among players of equal skill. It is not true in professional gambling, where overhead and profit must be paid at your expense; and it is not true for insurance, for precisely the same reason.

The premium you will pay for the liability policy will have to include something for sales costs, overhead, return on investment, and such things, then. This will have to be added to the average expectation—which is already greater than your own individual expectation as a good driver covering relatively few miles.

Thus the premium on your policy may easily be twice the expectation—on the face of it a poor gamble from your point of view although a splendid one from the company's.

Should you buy the policy anyway?

The answer comes down to what you can afford. Unless you are a very rich man, you probably can't afford to run even a tiny risk of a very large judgment. Nor do you wish to run the slightest chance of causing great damage to someone and being unable to pay for it.

You buy the liability policy.

Next you consider theft insurance, perhaps as the important element in a comprehensive policy that also covers fire and some minor risks. It happens that your hobby is working with delinquent boys. Because of this your car is habitually parked in areas where there is an exceptional likelihood of its being stolen.

From this you estimate that your expectation on this

policy is actually higher than the premium. You are a member of a special group which, over the years, will collect more from the company than the amount paid in premiums.

Even though theft of your car would not be a crippling disaster, you decide to take this policy. The odds are in your favor.

Finally you come to collision insurance. As a small-mileage, cautious driver you know the expectation is far less than the premium. You can well afford the cost of replacing your car if it is wrecked. Logically you decide against collision insurance.

But a little later you trade your old car in on a new model, jet-fendered, shiny, and expensive. Total destruction of this behemoth would put you in a difficult financial situation. So you feel you must insure it even though you will be paying perhaps $1 for each 50 cents' worth of expectation.

But then you find you must choose between $50-deductible and $100-deductible insurance, at a difference in premium of, say, $13. In four years the extra premium will amount to more than you will collect if you do have an accident.

Obviously you would be paying several times the expectation for this $50 worth of insurance against a hazard you could easily finance for yourself if the occasion should arise. Naturally you choose the $100-deductible policy instead, or a $200-deductible if you can find it.

In all these decisions you are following the wise rule of

insuring only against unbearable expenses except in the rare case where expectation exceeds cost.

What, by the way, is the difference between buying insurance and patronizing a gambling house—of the honest and legal variety found in, say, Las Vegas and Monte Carlo?

In gambling you know the odds or can easily learn them; in insurance they can at least be estimated. In both cases you have a losing expectation, since both kinds of institution must have rent and salary money and profits.

The difference, of course, lies in the nature of the contingency that leads to a payoff. In gambling it is arbitrary: you're as likely to win when you don't need the money as when you do. Insurance money, however, comes when you have sustained a loss and need it.

That's why insurance is often necessary and roulette is sometimes fun.

Besides being a source of pleasure to some and disaster to others, roulette is a splendid model for armchair study of the workings of probability theory. Such study, when undertaken at a safe distance from an actual wheel, can lead to an understanding of chance that is of real value when applied to many other phases of life.

It can also lead to an understanding of the realities of roulette. This is valuable too, since such understanding is enough to deter any sane man from playing wheels save for such stakes as he is prepared to lose.

For lose he must—mathematically speaking and in the long run.

A roulette wheel is a precision device for choosing at random among the 37 numbers from 0 to 36. Since half the numbers other than 0 are red and half are black, it also makes a random choice between these two colors.

Random means that it is precisely as likely that any one number or color will come up as another, although most people who play roulette wheels do not believe this, at least while they are playing.

A customer may bet on a number and have one chance in 37 of winning 35 times the amount he has staked plus his money back. If he should play one chip—call it $1 for convenience—on all 37 numbers, he would get the same result as he would get on the average by playing any sequence of 37 numbers on separate turns of the wheel. By doing this he would guarantee himself the same result in the short run that any play of single numbers would give him in a very long run.

In this instance he would put out $37. Since one of his numbers must win, he will get back $36.

From that his expectation is easy to figure. It is $36 for each $37 he plays, which gives him a long-run loss of 2.7% of whatever he stakes. It has been calculated that a steady player making $1 bets will lose at an average rate of $5.30 an hour.

It is also permissible to bet on two or more numbers at once, with exactly the same expectation.

All these figures, incidentally, apply to the kind of wheel used at Monte Carlo. The American wheel throws in 00 to make things tougher; and wheels with 000 are not un-

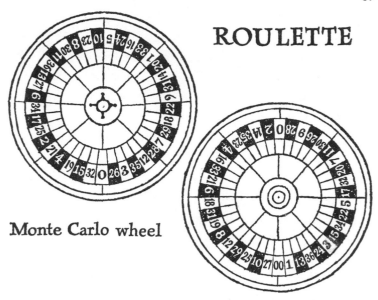

ROULETTE

Monte Carlo wheel

American wheel

known. But the principles are the same everywhere.

Most valuable of all in illustrating the workings of probability are the even chances. There are three such pairs offered, but an even chance is an even chance no matter what you call it, so let's stick to betting on red.

The rules say that if we bet $1 on red and it comes up, we win $1. If black comes we lose the dollar. If 0 comes we lose half our dollar. So what is the house percentage—the amount by which our expectation will be less than our stake?

If our wager is the equivalent of $1, we will receive back $2 on eighteen of the thirty-seven possibilities, and the equivalent of 50 cents on one of the thirty-seven. Our expectation is 18/37 of $2 plus 1/37 of 50 cents. This works out to about 98.65 cents per dollar, a house take of 1.35%. Not much, but it supports a glittering casino and is quite a help to the whole Principality of Monaco. *Fortune* magazine once figured that this 1.35% amounted up over the course of a year to a 125% return on invested capital.

There are three kinds of systems for beating the wheel: superstitious, mechanical, and mathematical.

Those of the first type use numerology, astrology, old telephone books, and dreams to choose between red and black or odd and even. Since it makes no predictable difference which of the even chances you select, these systems have no influence on results. They often make a player quite happy, though, while his luck lasts.

Mechanical systems depend upon your watching the dice or the wheel until you observe some kind of pattern in the numbers that come up, then betting on a continuation of that pattern. Such patterns do come up by the inevitable workings of chance, but they don't mean a thing . . . unless the wheel is imperfect.

Such a possibility is the basis of the widely quoted newspaper story about two college students who made a good deal of money in Reno. It seems they discovered an imperfect wheel on which one of the numbers came up more frequently than it should have. (There is also a rumor that the whole thing was a publicity stunt engineered by the house.)

Going back much further in time, there is some more encouragement for the observational school of system

players in the case of Charles Jaggers, a British engineer who detected a tiny flaw in a Monte Carlo wheel and won around $100,000. This, it is said, is what led to a routine of daily testing of all wheels with levels and calipers.

The main profit in mechanical systems, however, is the money you don't lose while you are too busy observing and tabulating to bet.

A variant is to find a wheel you are sure is dishonestly operated. Then place small bets on red, say, when there are large sums on black. You will have to be permitted to win your small bets so that the house can collect on the large ones. A defect in this system is that its use implies you believe the wheel crooked, and the proprietor is likely to resent the implication and personally throw you out of the place.

Doubling systems are something else again. They work, in a way and within certain limits. Most real system play is based on doubling.

The favorite is the martingale.* To follow it you simply bet some fixed sum, say $1, to begin with, and continue to bet that amount each time you win. But each time you lose, double your bet the next time. No matter when you quit and go home, just so long as it is following a win, you will be ahead of the game. Your profit will be as many dollars as you have had wins.

This method works equally well for coin-flipping or any other enterprise based on even chances.

It is mathematically sound in the sense that it has actually permitted you to be almost certain of a small gain. In return for this near-guarantee, however, you have accepted the tiny—but real—risk of a large loss.

For an example, take a look at the results of eight actual games shown on the next five pages. These were coin-tossing games of twenty plays each. Betting was always on heads to win. Use of the martingale system gave heavy odds in favor of winning each game. The risk was that a run of tails at the end of any game would bring about a heavy loss.

Limiting these games to a fixed number of plays produced a situation equivalent to that commonly met in gambling, where there is risk of a heavy loss for a slightly different reason.

---

* The word's a bit of a mystery. It may come from a Spanish—originally Arabic—word for a rein, since the word *martingale* still most often refers to the strap that keeps a horse from rearing or tossing his head. A system has somewhat the same effect on a player.

The intelligent citizen's guide to
MARTINGALE

I THINK I'LL PLAY A FEW GAMES JUST FOR LAUGHS!

Game No. 1

	Bet	Result	Won	Lost	Total
Place a $1 bet →	1	T		1	−1
Double every time you lose →	2	H	2		+1
Bet $1 every time you win →	1	T		1	0
Double →	2	H	2		+2
	1	T		1	+1
Double →	2	H	2		+3
	1	H	1		+4
	1	T		1	+3
Double →	2	T		2	+1
Double again →	4	H	4		+5
	1	H	1		+6
	1	T		1	+5
Double →	2	T		2	+3
Double again →	4	T		4	−1
... and again →	8	T		8	−9
... and still again →	16	H	16		+7
	1	H	1		+8
Bet $1 every time you win →	1	H	1		+9
	1	H	1		+10
	1	T		1	+9

Net after 1ˢᵗ game of 20 tosses → ## $9 ahead

Game No. 2

Bet	Result	Won	Lost	Total
1	H	1		+1
1	H	1		+2
1	T		1	+1
2	H	2		+3
1	H	1		+4
1	T		1	+3
2	H	2		+5
1	H	1		+6
1	T		1	+5
2	H	2		+7
1	H	1		+8
1	T		1	+7
2	H	2		+9
1	H	1		+10
1	H	1		+11
1	H	1		+12
1	H	1		+13
1	T		1	+12
2	T		2	+10
4	H	4		+14

Game No. 3

Bet	Result	Won	Lost	Total
1	H	1		+1
1	T		1	0
2	H	2		+2
1	H	1		+3
1	T		1	+2
2	T		2	0
4	H	4		+4
1	H	1		+5
1	H	1		+6
1	H	1		+7
1	T		1	+6
2	H	2		+8
1	H	1		+9
1	T		1	+8
2	H	2		+10
1	H	1		+11
1	H	1		+12
1	T		1	+11
2	T		2	+9
4	H	4		+13

$23 ahead

WHAT CAN I LOSE?

$36 ahead

IT'S ONLY AN EXPERIMENT— 34, 35, 36.

Game No. 4

Bet	Result	Won	Lost	Total
1	T		1	-1
2	T		2	-3
4	T		4	-7
8	T		8	-15
16	H	16		+1
1	H	1		+2
1	H	1		+3
1	H	1		+4
1	T		1	+3
2	H	2		+5
1	H	1		+6
1	T		1	+5
2	H	2		+7
1	T		1	+6
2	T		2	+4
4	T		4	0
8	T		8	-8
16	T			-24
32	H	32		+8
1	H	1		+9

Game No. 5

Bet	Result	Won	Lost	Total
1	T		1	-1
2	H	2		+1
1	T		1	0
2	H	2		+2
1	H	1		+3
1	H	1		+4
1	T		1	+3
2	T		2	+1
4	T		4	-3
8	H	8		+5
1	T		1	+4
2	H	2		+6
1	H	1		+7
1	T		1	+6
2	H	2		+8
1	H	1		+9
1	T		1	+8
2	H	2		+10
1	T		1	+9
2	H	2		+11

$45 ahead

A PERFECTLY LOGICAL SYSTEM—

$56 ahead

SMALL STEADY GAINS ARE BALANCED BY—

Game No. 6

Bet	Result	Won	Lost	Total
1	H	1		+1
1	T		1	0
2	H	2		+2
1	H	1		+3
1	H	1		+4
1	H	1		+5
1	T		1	+4
2	H	2		+6
1	T		1	+5
2	H	2		+7
1	T		1	+6
2	H	2		+8
1	H			+9
1	T		1	+8
2	T		2	+6
4	H	4		+10
1	T		1	+9
2	H	2		+11
1	T		1	+10
2	T		2	+8

Game No. 7

Bet	Result	Won	Lost	Total
1	T		1	-1
2	T		2	-3
4	T		4	-7
8	H	8		+1
1	T		1	·0
2	H			+2
1	T		1	+1
2	T		2	-1
4	H	4		+3
1	T		1	+2
2	T		2	0
4	H	4		+4
1	T		1	+3
2	T		2	+1
4	H	4		+5
1	T		1	+4
2	T		2	+2
4	H	4		+6
1	H	1		+7
1	H	1		+8

$64 ahead

$72 ahead

A REMOTE CHANCE OF HEAVY LOSSES.

I'LL TAKE THAT RISK.

Game No. 8

Bet	Result	Won	Lost	Total
1	H	1		+1
1	H	1		+2
1	H	1		+3
1	T		1	+2
2	T		2	0
4	T		4	-4
8	H	8		+4
1	T		1	+3
2	T		2	+1
4	T		4	-3
8	H	8		+5
1	T		1	+4
2	H	2		+6
1	T		1	+5
2	T		2	+3
4	T		4	-1
8	T		8	-9
16	T		16	-25
32	T		32	-57
64	T		64	-121

$49 in the hole

OF ALL THE ROTTEN CRUMMY LUCK!

The reason: you may be forced to break the rule of quitting only after a win. This will happen if a series of losses followed by doubling each time brings you to a wager larger than your capital or larger than the limit placed by the house. Maybe it's what was in Thackeray's mind when he had a character say, "You have not played as yet? Do not do so; above all avoid a martingale if you do."

Not even a well-backed martingale can change the expectation of the game. You will still lose 1.35% of your wagered money in the long run at roulette, if you play the even chances on a one–zero wheel, double that if it is the American kind. And you will still break exactly even in the long run at home-style coin-tossing.

Possibly you would prefer a game in which you are extremely likely to lose a small amount but have a small chance of winning a very large sum. You can convert roulette into such a game by using the system called an anti-martingale.

Mathematically you thus have the equivalent of disaster insurance or a lottery. For a few dollars you can insure yourself against the expense of a costly disease if it is a rare one. A $1 lottery ticket may give you one chance in a million of winning $100,000 plus slightly greater chances of winning somewhat smaller sums.

To play an anti-martingale you select the number of successive wins you are prepared to gamble for. You might make it eleven, the longest *paroli* that is permitted under the limit used in some gambling establishments.

You quit as soon as you lose once—or when you have won eleven times in a row if this is your lucky night. If you lose, you lose $1. If you win, you win $2,047.

That sounds favorable, but the expectation remains the same—a long-run loss on your part of 1.35% of what you have risked. You will be a $1 loser more than 2,047 times as often as you will be a $2,047 winner.

The point to all this, of course, is not so much how to play roulette as to recognize how in any chance situation you can swap probabilities around. And you can never change the mathematical expectation. In the nature of things it will always be contrived to favor the house—or the insurance company.

Optimists and others wishing to justify their gambling as rational if not moral may like to point to the case of Charles Wells, immortalized in song as "the man who broke the bank at Monte Carlo."

Mr. Wells, an Englishman, didn't exactly break the bank, which has millions of dollars at its command, but he did clean out all the money available at one table. He won close to $200,000 in three days of eleven-hour sessions. (He went back later and lost most of it.)

If such a win is against all odds, how could Wells do it? Doesn't his triumph suggest there is something wrong in the predictions made from probability theory?

Actually, it points up one of the basic principles, which is that every conceivable sequence is as likely as any other.

If, as has been remarked, enough apes were given enough typewriters and banged them at random long enough, they might eventually write all the books in the British Museum. In a very large number of attempts, every pattern of letters and spaces would probably occur, including the one that is this chapter.

Production of this chapter might take a while that way, though. Let's see. Figure that these 3,000-odd words add up to 20,000 letters and spaces. Assume a typewriter that permits the ape to choose among 26 letters and 14 other characters, for spacing, numbers, and punctuation.

Even something less than a book or a chapter, the mere salutation to a business letter, makes a monumental typing problem for monkeys, a situation illustrated here.

The first letter of this chapter is P. There is one chance in 40 that our assiduous ape will hit it, and the same goes for each other letter, number, or space in the chapter. So the chance he will hit the precise key 20,000 times consecutively is one in $40^{20,000}$, a number much too large to comprehend directly. It is much greater than one physicist's calculation of the number of electrons making up the universe, although it is not anything like so large as the total possible number of moves in a game of chess.

All in all, you can see why the publisher of this volume goes on paying royalties to human authors instead of acquiring a stable of apes.

Sir Arthur Eddington had his own way of putting the whole idea:

> There once was a brainy baboon
> Who always breathed down a bassoon,
>   For he said, "It appears
>   That in billions of years
> I shall certainly hit on a tune."

d

By chance, one monkey should average one "d" a minute.

dear

Three monkeys should achieve a "dear" every ten weeks.

dear sir

10,000 of 'em will average one "dear sir" per 150 years.

CHAPTER 3

The Difficulties of Probability

STATISTICAL	INDUCTIVE
Means relative frequency	Means weighing the evidence
probably (1 chance in 4) he will get the plaid tie.	*probably it will rain.*

*The two kinds of probability,
the controversy over them, and how we
often go wrong in thinking about chance.*

WE HAVE been pretending so far that probability theory is a cut-and-dried thing, all of a piece, and beyond argument. In fact, however, it is one of the liveliest scientific debating topics of the day, under verbal fire from many quarters.

To smooth out the contradictions in this, let's start by noting that a theory of this kind isn't simply true or false. It is rather a model of reality—a good model as long as (and where) it is useful, a bad model when extended beyond that point.

Scientific thinkers have given us, and themselves, all sorts of models of the real world. Very useful they can be, too. Euclid's geometry is one, and Newton's physics is another. Einstein and others have come along to show us where these models become misleading and we cry in our disillusion that they are false theories. But they are still as "true" (as useful, as workable) as ever where they do fit. And all is well so long as scientists don't, as artists sometimes do, become too attached to their models.

Try this one. If you say to a friend, "Think of a number from one to ten," what's the probability he'll name any given number? One in ten? The model, the basics of probability, seems to say so. In fact, he is more likely to name 3 or 7 than any of the others, presumably because of the many connotations these numbers have picked up over the centuries. The model then does not apply, and it is very important to keep this sort of instance in mind. You'll meet more of its kind in this book, especially in the chapter about extrasensory perception.

The rules of probability often help in correcting other models that are being extended beyond their utility. When a physician falls into the error of treating "an average man" instead of the patient who really is before him, his model needs this kind of correction.

People are diverse. A chemist has noted that from one person to another the amount of alkaline phosphatase in the blood varies in an elevenfold range, arginase fourfold, cholinesterase threefold, beta-glucuronidase thirtyfold; and all are important body-controlling chemicals.

Stomachs vary in size by fifteen to one; hearts by two to one in size, three to one in pumping rate. Define a medium-sized organ as one in the middle one-third of the range, consider only eight of our many organs, and it still turns out that only one person in 6,500 is "medium" in this

It feems that everyone is a little Queer except ME and THEE and fometimes I think even THEE is a little Queer.

respect. So says Dr. Roger J. Williams, one of the discoverers of vitamins.

(This is multiplication of probabilities again. Multiply together the 1/3 chance for each organ eight times and you'll get approximately 1/6,500.)

In support of this diversity principle, one doctor has offered the case of a man who drank a quart of scotch whisky every day for 60 years, yet managed a successful business almost until his death at 93. No constitution of ordinary enzyme efficiency could have managed the job.

For clarity, imagine a dozen men: All are of average height, give or take an inch or two; they have normal amounts of hair, wear size 8 to 9 shoes, share only a slight tendency to put on weight, own average sexual impulses, digestive systems, vision, hearing, and in fact all other characteristics.

Now imagine another dozen: On the *average,* they have about the same height, vision, and so on as the first group. But among them is a six-foot-sixer and a five-footer, a pair of myopics, a manic-depressive, and an alcoholic. One's fat, two are thin, and the shapes of their feet vary a good deal.

The second group has problems the first group would never know, from difficulty in finding a comfortable hotel bed or shopping for shoes, to a long range of medical and dental problems.

The point to this, and it affects all who deal with people, is that human beings generally resemble the second group much more closely than they do the first. When medical men take the first group as their model they fail to confront, much less solve, most basic problems.

To work our way gently from this model to what it means, and what *we* mean, when we talk in terms of probability or chance, let's consider a few specific problems.

If you have four neckties—spotted, plaid, striped, plain —on a rack and choose one blindly, what's the probability it'll be the plaid?

Three men give their hats to a hat-check girl without receiving checks. What's the chance she'll later return the right hats to the right men, assuming there are no other customers and that she makes no use of eye or brain?

If you go fox-hunting tomorrow, will you shoot a fox? You might answer "Probably" or "Probably not," depending partly upon your knowledge of the circumstances and partly upon your temperament or your mood of the moment. You may feel you have given a reasonably good indication of the probability as you see it. But perhaps you have not. Such words as these are not merely imprecise; they actually mean different things to different people.

Pinned down then, you may finally say, "I'd give myself one chance in three." And now at least you will be correctly understood.

A weather forecaster announces a 30-percent chance of rain tomorrow.

Your doctor gives you a 50-50 chance of coming through an operation.

These instances will help to illustrate the different ways in which mathematical philosophers, as well as scientists who use the concepts of probability in their work, have viewed this debated subject.

One way is statistical. One chance in four that you'll select the plaid cravat means simply that out of a large number of draws in identical circumstances one-fourth will turn out plaid.

The hat-check puzzle is a little more involved, but it is

still a good statistical instance. Repeat the experiment many times and it will come out right one-sixth of the time.*

Or take a look at the pictorial version of this situation. There are six different ways that three hats will fit three heads. Two times out of six everybody has the wrong hat. Half the time only one is rightly hatted. And once in six times everybody's as he should be.

The fox-hunting question begins to edge out of the statistical situation into what has usually been called inductive probability. You are only going hunting once, perhaps, so what does it mean to say that you will get a fox one time in three? And you won't get one-third of a fox. You'll either get a whole fox or none.

So it is with the weather. It will rain or it won't.

You'll survive the operation, which is unique, or you will die.

An inductive probability may be thought of as strength of conviction. At most times your belief that it will rain tomorrow is more intense, as one writer has pointed out, than your belief that the roof above you will collapse. You believe you may be hit by a car as you cross the street, but you believe more strongly that you will cross safely.

Our inductive probabilities—fox, rain, surgery—become clearer when thought of as odds. If forced to place a bet

* The chance the first man will get the proper one of the three hats is one in three. The chance the second will get his hat of the remaining two is one in two. With only one man and one hat remaining, last fellow's chance is one in one. Multiply one-third by one-half by one to get one-sixth, or one chance in six.

on one of them, the chances given would be the fairest
odds for you on either side of the wager.

Thus, through numbers or odds, inductive probabilities
become at least analogous to statistical probabilities. They
are not the same thing, but they can be thought about and
worked with in the same numerical terms. And that is
about as close as we are likely to get here to reconciling
these kinds of probability which are being fiercely argued
now, as they have been from time to time almost since the
idea of mathematical probability was born.

The first major treatise on probability dates back to the
early 1700's. Jakob Bernoulli, one of a great Swiss family
of mathematicians, saw it as "The Art of Conjecture."
Pierre de Laplace, French mathematician and astronomer,
agreed a century later that the utility of probability theory
was to guide us in weighing assumptions.

Since then, and right down to today, probability has generally been given a statistical interpretation.

A great exception was the work of John Maynard
Keynes, whose thinking on economics changed the lives
of all of us (there was a lot of Keynes in the New Deal).
He rejected the statistical concept in his "Treatise on
Probability" in 1921. He argued, with considerable influence, that all statements of probability could be best
handled in inductive terms.

In our own decade, Rudolf Carnap has made the most
productive effort to reconcile the two ideas. He sees
statistical probability as valuable for describing a situation, inductive probability for making judgments about

such statements.

However, some of the latest and liveliest research has nothing to do with either of these probabilities, but with the human side. Is one man's probability another's?

Obviously, not always. That's what makes betting, just as differences of opinion are said to be what make horse races.

You roll a die twice, and twice it comes up three.

The man on your left has certain vague and inaccurate, but widely held, ideas about what "the law of averages says." He knows that in the long run a three should be no more frequent than any other of the five numbers, so he is prepared to bet on any number against a three for the next roll. Things must balance out, he feels, and it is some other number's turn to come up.

The man on your right believes in lucky streaks, a prevalence of runs. It is a theory on which elaborate and published systems of gambling have been based. He will offer better than one to five on another three.

Opposite you is a man of mathematical mind. He believes in neither hot streaks nor maturity of chances. He contends that the chance of another three is just exactly as good as for any other one number, and he will bet on one as willingly as another, if he bothers to bet at all.

You, however, have reason to suspect the die has been tampered with—loaded or shaved. This leads you to believe it now has a bias, and the history of two tosses suggest a bias favoring threes.

But lounging across the way is still another fellow. He is the one who loaded the die. He loaded it to favor the six and secretly tested it by a series of several hundred tosses in which six came up nearly half the time. He is prepared to bet that the chance of a six on the next toss is almost one in two.

For each of you there is a different probability for the same toss of the same die. This is what is called subjective probability. It depends upon the state of your information and, at the same time, upon your emotional makeup and condition.

How people think about probability is a useful study in understanding them and working with them—and yourself. In investigations of subjective probability at the University of Manchester, John Cohen faced children with sets of choices involving the laws of chance. He found some interesting parallels to the ways all of us behave.

He showed children aged ten to sixteen a bowl of beads,

explaining it contained blue and yellow ones in equal numbers. Then he put four beads, drawn at random from the bowl, into each of sixteen cups. The children were asked to guess how many of the cups would contain each of the five possible combinations.

The best the youngest children could do was guess that the combinations were not all equally likely. Those a little older began to suspect two and two would be the most probable combination. Somewhat older ones could see that one blue and three yellow beads would be as likely as one yellow and three blue. The oldest children recognized four of a color as the least likely of combinations.

It is possibly encouraging to see that as children grow older they bring their judgments of chance situations closer and closer to mathematical expectation—in other words, closer to reality.

Professor Cohen and his associates also tested estimates of probability among bus drivers—old hands and beginners starting training. The test: how narrow a gap the driver thought he could bring his unwieldy double-decker through. It turned out that the most experienced drivers almost never assumed a probability of success with gaps which were in fact too narrow. The beginners frequently did. Some useful conclusions about automobile driving, and perhaps other human activities, might be drawn.

There are two efforts that any person could make in attempting to cope with chance situations. The first is to bring his information to a maximum. The second is to bring an understanding of the laws of probability to bear in

forming his subjective probability; and some of the other Manchester experiments suggest how most people fail in this.

Suppose you may draw once for the one lucky ticket in a box of 10. Or draw ten times for the single lucky ticket in a box of 100, replacing the ticket each time before drawing again.

Cohen found that about four people out of five preferred the single draw, although the mathematical chances are identical.

They held to this choice even when offered as many as fifty draws from the box of 100, an overwhelmingly better bet.

Contrarily (and that's the word for it) a few people seemed to regard two chances as better than one, no matter how slight each of the two might be. For them, two draws from a box of 100 seemed better than one draw from a box of 10 . . . a choice of a 2-percent chance over a 10-percent one.

It also appears that even intelligent adults confuse addition with multiplication of probabilities. Given a choice between a single one-chance-in-ten situation and three of one-in-three (in which all must succeed or failure is total), many will choose the latter.

A general with such views might commit himself to three battles in each of which he had a one-third chance and all of which he must win to complete the campaign successfully. He would prefer the series to a single one-chance-in-ten battle. Yet his chance of winning all three would be the product of the three fractions ($1/3 \times 1/3 \times 1/3$) or a slim one chance in 27.

CHAPTER 4

The Dice That Started It All

*The Chevalier de Méré,
a crapshooter, writes a letter
of inquiry to Blaise Pascal,
mathematician and mystic.*

THE PAIR of dice that had been winning money for the Chevalier de Méré began to lose it for him even faster, so he wrote a letter to a friend.

Because this seventeenth-century letter was addressed to Blaise Pascal, mathematician and philosopher, it launched the history of the calculus of probability. In finding the answer to de Méré's puzzle, Pascal began an inquiry into the principles of chance and probability. In letters of his own, he took up the problems with Pierre de Fermat. Parliamentary Town Councillor of Toulouse and by trade a lawyer, Fermat was nevertheless a major figure in several fields of mathematics. What this series of letters started has grown into the science of probability and the art of statistics.

The Chevalier de Méré had done very well for himself over a period of time by betting that he could get at least one six in four rolls of a die. It seemed reasonable to him that this bet should win more often than it should lose, and the growing health of his purse confirmed his faith in his own logic.

The wager that initiated the study of mathematical probability by threatening to impoverish the Chevalier in 1654 was something else again, although it is not surprising that in the absence of such theory he regarded it as a good investment. For some reason, possibly because he had run out of takers for his other wager, de Méré had switched to betting that within a sequence of 24 tosses of a pair of dice he would roll at least one 12. He had learned, somewhat bitterly, that he could afford to make such a bet only with odds in his favor. At even money, it was a loser. But what odds, exactly? Or increase the tosses to how many for a fair bet?

In the absence of a method of calculating probability, de Méré could answer these financially pressing questions only by the tedious method of making a very large number of throws and then studying the record or hefting his pocketbook. For, alas, as Pascal pointed out in gentle rebuke, de Méré, though a fine fellow, was no mathematician. "This is, as you know, a great fault," added Pascal in discussing de Méré with Fermat.

THE CHEVALIER de MÉRÉ
PROBABLY LOOKED LIKE THIS

I. GEIS *del. 1909*

It is apparent that on his first type of wager, de Méré could begin by figuring that he had an equal chance of rolling any one of the six numbers on the die on his first throw, assuming an honest cube, well-made and undoctored. The likelihood of a six, as of any other number, then was 1/6 on each throw.

For four throws it might seem that the chance would be four times as good, for a probability of 4/6 or 2/3. This would tell de Méré that he would win two wagers for every one he would lose and virtually assure him of heavy profits. This calculation and the conclusion it leads to are wrong.

Before straightening out the matter, let's see where it misleads us in the case of the Chevalier's second bet.

Since dice are cubes offering the numbers from one to six, it is possible to obtain a 12 only when both dice come up 6 on the same toss. Since each will do so once in six times, the probability is 1/6 times 1/6, or 1/36, for each toss of two dice. So far the logic is good.

The fallacy comes in multiplying 1/36 by 24 and saying that in 24 tosses the chance of a 12 coming up at least once is 24/36 or 2/3. This false trail leads to a conclusion that the second bet is exactly as overwhelmingly good as the first. As de Méré discovered, it is not.

It is easy to demonstrate that something is wrong with this reasoning. Apply it to the first instance and it will tell you that for six rolls instead of four the probability of at least one six is 6/6 or 1—that is, that in a series of six rolls there will always be at least one six. It's true that this is the average number you will get, but in some of the groups of six rolls obviously there will be no sixes, just as in others there will be two or more.

To find out the true expectation of these "at least once" problems, it is most productive to approach them backwards. All the contingencies in any case must add up to 1, or certainty, which here is a statement that each roll will either be a 6 or it will not. So we can discover the probability of a six by finding first the probability that there will be no sixes in the sequence and then subtracting this fraction from 1.

Since there is only 1 chance in 6 of success on each roll, there are 5 in 6 of failure—a failure probability of 5/6. Take 5/6 four times, once for each toss allowed. Multiply these fractions by each other and you get 625/1296 or about 13/27. This being the chance of failure, 14/27 is the probability of success. Odds favoring the Chevalier's first bet actually were 14 to 13, not nearly so good as it at first appeared but quite good enough. They are, in fact, about fifty percent better than those that amply support the roulette wheel at Monte Carlo today and more than twice as good as those that favor the house in a crap game.

But for the disillusioned Chevalier's second bet we must take his chance of failing to throw 12 on any one toss, which is 35/36, and multiply together 24 of these fractions for the 24 times he is allowed to toss. When this fraction is subtracted from 1 we discover that the bet that looked so good to de Méré would in fact lose slightly more often than it would win.

The little cubes that in the hands of de Méré gave rise to such an important branch, and tool, of science were an old toy even then. Their way of combining chance with predictability made them an early part of the ideas of divination and destiny and justice.

In some mythologies the course of the world is seen as determined by dice cast in higher places—by the Ases of Eddic mythology, by Shiva with his queen, in the Iliad by

THE ANCIENT ART
OF CONTROLLING RANDOMIZING CUBES

Poseidon, Zeus, and Hades. It appears possible that gambling, ancient though it is, may have grown out of the use of dice and comparable apparatus for divination in times of distress or dispute.

Many primitive peoples, including the Maoris, cast lots to find out a criminal. Rabelais, too, found virtue of a sort in randomized decision; his Judge Bridlegoose decided lawsuits by throwing dice and was famous for his fairness and wisdom until failing eyesight prevented him from reading the spots accurately.

It was the Marquis de Condorcet, however, who had more serious hopes of seeing the theories of probability put to work to improve courts of law. His ideas offer a nice example of what probability theory cannot do for the world. Each court, he suggested, should be made up of so large a number of judges that violent and prejudiced opinions would be balanced out. Sad to say, Condorcet himself eventually came before a French court made up of a large number of judges. It was a revolutionary tribunal, the judges held a body of extreme views in common, and Condorcet went to the guillotine.

Gamblers are inclined to put an equally misplaced faith in what they conceive to be the laws of probability. Any man while gambling is likely to respond primitively. He may believe simultaneously in the contradictory fallacies of catching a run of luck while it is hot and of taking advantage of the "maturity of chances."

In one moment he bets on the number or the player that has won several times in a row. The dice, he says, are hot.

Or the player is in the midst of a lucky streak. But, in fact, dice have no memories and luck is of no use in predicting the future but only in describing the past.

A newspaper story tells of a pair of dice enthroned on red velvet behind glass in the lobby of the Desert Inn at Las Vegas. With this pair a young man made 28 straight passes in 1950. Since the player was reluctant to parlay his winnings his profit was only $750, but the house lost about $150,000 to what the newspaper describes as "shrewd onlookers making side bets." But were they shrewd, except by hindsight?

The denial of luck that makes a man "shrewd" if he has won is common among men when they gamble. Eighty years ago a discerning Englishman recognized and described these feelings in himself while at Monte Carlo:

. . . when I succeeded I raked up my gains, with a half impression that I had been a clever fellow, and had made a judicious stake, just as if I had really moved a skilful move at chess; and that when I failed, I thought to myself, "Ah, I knew all the time I was going wrong in selecting that number, and yet I was fool enough to stick to it," which was, of course, a pure illusion, for all that I did know the chance was even, or much more than even against me. But this illusion followed me throughout. I had a sense of *deserving* success when I succeeded, or of having failed through my own wilfulness, or wrong-headed caprice, when I failed.

The favored obeisance to dice today is made at craps, and its rules are quite widely known, though the working of the odds perhaps is not.

The shooter rolls two dice, after the bet is offered and

accepted. If the points add up to 7 or 11 he wins at once; if 2, 3, or 12 he loses. Any other total neither wins nor loses but becomes the shooter's point. He continues to roll until he either repeats his point, and wins, or throws a 7, and loses.

Craps, as well as being a popular method for the exchange of money, offers many illustrations of the calculus of chance of somewhat greater complexity than in coin-tossing. Just what are the odds for or against the shooter?

EIGHT WAYS TO MAKE A NATURAL

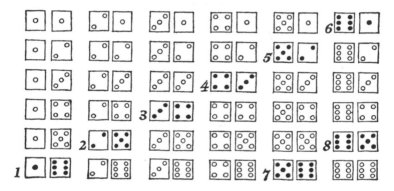

There are the usual 36 possible combinations on each toss—6 for one die times 6 for the other. Six of the 36 add up to 7 (6 and 1, 1 and 6, 5 and 2, 2 and 5, 4 and 3, 3 and 4), and two add up to 11. So the shooter can expect to win 8 times in 36 with a natural.

There is one way of making a 2, two ways of making a 3, one way of getting a 12. The shooter will lose at once 4 times in 36.

If neither of these sets of possibilities occurs, the shooter's chance of repeating his point depends upon what it is, but the chance is never as good as even. Seven comes up more frequently than either 4, 5, 6, 8, 9, or 10. The likelihood of getting a 4, for instance, before a 7 is 1 in 3.

The chance of throwing a 4 in the first place is 3 in 36. This multiplied by the 1/3 chance of then throwing it ahead of a 7 gives a probability of 1/36.

Figure the probabilities similarly for the other five possible points. Add these six fractions to the 8/36 chance of a natural in the first place and you will have 244/495.

This is the shooter's chance of winning, figured from the beginning of the game. In decimal form it is .49293, which means that in the long run the shooter will come out with a loss of 1.41% of the money he has bet.

This explains why, in a gambling establishment, it is always the customer who shoots and never the house. And why the informed bettor always wagers against the shooter in making side bets unless he can get odds good enough to overbalance the probability of losing.

CHAPTER 5

Why the Fire Tongs Burned Your Hand

And the probability,
atoms and molecules
being the way they are,
that this book is about
to leap into the air.

IF YOU hold one end of a fire tongs in a hot blaze long enough, the other end will probably burn your hand. Not surely, only probably, but so very probably that you are quite safe in neglecting the alternate chance.

To see why *probably* instead of *surely*, and to see why it happens at all, calls for a look at the way modern physics regards heat or thermal motion.

More than a century ago an English botanist named Robert Brown noticed that tiny plant spores are often kicked violently about by some invisible force. This

Brownian motion is to be seen in small organisms floating in liquids and in particles of dust and smoke in the air. It is a result of kicks by molecules, which are in constant and violent motion. Heat the liquid and the motion increases in vigor. Cool it to $-273°$ C., which we call absolute zero, and all the molecules will come to rest.

This thermal motion is completely irregular. You can no more predict the behavior of any molecule than you can which side of a tossed coin will turn up. But, as with a great number of coins flipped at once, the total effect can be forecast on the basis of probability. It is subject to a new kind of law, which is sometimes called the Law of Disorder or the Law of Statistical Behavior.

There is an old and famous problem that makes it easier to understand this form of prediction-by-probability. It's called the Drunkard's Walk.

The drunk in this story is leaning against a lamp post—naturally—in the center of the town square. He decides to walk, although in his condition he really doesn't care where he goes. He takes a few steps this way, a few steps that, changing course perhaps every three feet in a discouragingly random way.

After, say, a hundred of these zigs and zags, how far from the lamp post will our cheerful traveler be?

This may sound totally unpredictable, and for any *one* drunk it very nearly is, though even for him the one most likely distance can be calculated. With some help from Pythagoras and his square on the hypotenuse (this is not the same square the drunk is wandering in) we find that

THE DRUNKARD'S WALK

the most probable distance the drunkard will be from the lamp post after a number of zigzags is equal to the average length of each zig or zag multiplied by the square root of their number.

After one hundred staggers averaging 3 feet each, he will most probably be only 30 feet on his way. This indicates the advantages of sobriety for pedestrians.

Any one drunk, or any one molecule, may end up anywhere; but, drunks or molecules, there is a predictable average about which their behavior will tend to group. If our drunk were to pursue his hundred-stagger course each night for many years and mark his end point with a cross each time, the greatest number of these crosses would eventually be seen to form the circumference of a circle of 30-foot radius around the lamp.

If the number of drunkard's trips were very large, as is the number of molecules in a drop of water, we could predict this pattern very precisely and be almost—though never quite—sure we would be right.

To see what happens you might gently pour a little clear water on top of a half-glass of water tinted a beautiful purple with some potassium permanganate. How long will it take for the two to mix?

Each molecule of the coloring matter will take part in a trillion consecutive collisions in each second, moving one one-hundred-millionth of an inch each time. The rule of the drunkard says that we may find the average net distance by multiplying the distance of each movement by the square root of their number. The average speed of diffusion then comes out one one-hundredth of an inch per second.

After 10,000 seconds, the color will have moved 100 (the square root of 10,000) times further, or about an inch. Since this is nearly three hours, you can see the advantage of stirring a drink if you're in any kind of hurry.

This brings us back to the tongs that probably burned your hand. A poker might seem a more reasonable example, but the word poker will appear all too many times in this book anyway. So—it's a tongs that you put in the fire to illustrate the connection between probability theory and the laws of thermodynamics.

The difference between your heated tongs and a piece of glass or other relatively poor conductor is that the atoms of a metal lose some of their outer electrons, which dash about in irregular thermal motion. This activity is greatly increased as the end of the tongs is heated, so the molecules begin to diffuse along the tongs, carrying with them the extra energy of the heat.

The progress toward burning your hand will follow the same laws of probability that govern the tinted water and the drunkard in the town square.

That is why your blister is not a sure thing but merely a probability, though by odds of billions of billions to one and then some.

Now consider the sun. In its lively interior, energy is liberated as intense radiation, which heads for the surface at what we know as the speed of light—186,000 miles per second. With a mere 420,000 miles (the radius of the sun) to go, it should arrive in a few seconds. Instead it takes hundreds of years, on the average. The light quanta move in drunkard's steps.

They take part in a great number of collisions with atoms and electrons, progressing only about one centimeter per bounce on the average. To reach the surface, a matter of some 70 billion centimeters, the number of drunkard's steps required is the square of 70 billion,* then; and even though a light quantum can manage 30 billion

* Which works out, just to give an idea of the kind of numbers we are so glibly dealing with, to about fifty times one mathematician's estimate of the number of grains of sand making up the beach at Coney Island.

bounces to the second, this comes out a 5,000-year journey.

After all those centuries, however, the energy can make it the vastly longer rest of the way to the earth in only eight seconds. This illustrates even more impressively than the drunkard did the value of a direct route.

Even the blue of the sky that delights our eyes is a product, and evidence, of the random behavior of matter. It is the chance fluctuation of the density of the atmosphere that scatters blue rays in the spectrum. Without this we'd have a jet-black sky in which stars could be seen shining all day. It would be an astronomer's dream. It will come true when scientists succeed in putting a telescope into orbit up there.

The air in the room in which you are sitting now varies in its density from place to place as chance produces a greater concentration of molecules in one region and then another. The half of the room you are occupying may quite suddenly become devoid of air one minute from now, to your considerable disadvantage. This is clearly possible, since each of the molecules has an even chance of sharing your half of the room with you—and an equal chance of fleeing to the other.

The odds are rather in your favor, of course. They are the same as those against your getting all heads should you now flip a number of pennies equal to the number of molecules of air in the room. Even if the room were a vessel like the one pictured, so tiny as to contain only a hundred molecules, this event would occur once in every few million billion years on the average. For a vessel of ordinary size (to say nothing of a room), with its trillions of mole-

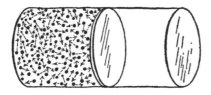

All molecules of air are now in the vessel's left compartment.

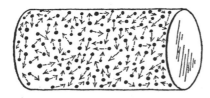

Remove the partition — By random motion the molecules of air spread throughout the vessel.

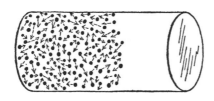

What is the probability that for an instant all of the molecules will be on one side?

cules, the event is incomparably more remote. The monkeys of a few chapters back should turn out their library of books far sooner.

Now about the book you are holding. It is being bombarded by air molecules from all sides, and so long as these pressures remain reasonably equal, gravity keeps it down. But some day, surely, if you and the book and the air can hold out long enough, by chance there will come an instant when very many molecules strike from below and only a few from above. This book will leap from your hand.

But what are the odds? Or to put it differently, once in how many years on the average will this shocking bit of poltergeistery occur? Not as often as once in a googol of years but more often than once in a googolplex, say Edward Kasner and James Newman in *Mathematics and the Imagination*. In planning for this event you may want to know that a googol is the number 1 followed by one-hundred zeros. (The number of electrons in the universe is estimated at less than a googol.) And a googolplex is 1 followed by a googol of zeros.

The book will surely rise one day. Meanwhile, don't hold your breath waiting.

These bits about the behavior of particles illustrate the way in which the new physics views the universe. Probability was at first most often regarded as a makeshift way in which to look at nature until the day when we could truly understand her laws. Today's view is much more that expressed by Charles G. Darwin: "The uncertainties of the world we now ascribe not to the uncertainties of our thoughts, but rather to the character of the world around us. It is a more sensible, more mature and more comprehensible view."

It is also a useful one, as in the case of what is somewhat luridly known as the Monte Carlo Method. It is a trick for tying the newly recognized random behavior of basic particles to one of the older devices for producing random numbers—the roulette wheel. What it uses in actual practice is a truly superwheel, the electronic calculator.

The problem rose at Los Alamos when it became vitally important to discover the amount of shielding needed for human safety in the vicinity of atomic fission. And there was an understandable reluctance to wait for experience or trial and error to come up with an answer.

The roulette-wheel solution was provided by two mathematicians, the late John von Neumann and Stanislaus Ulam. (We'll see a good deal more in a later chapter of how von Neumann studied the probabilities of life with the help of games and gambling.)

A typical question in a place like Los Alamos is this: What percentage of the neutrons in a certain beam will get through this tank of water without being absorbed or losing most of their speed? The Monte Carlo approach is to trace by probabilities the histories of each of a rather large sample of the neutrons making up the beam as they wander through the water, colliding now and then with a hydrogen or oxygen nucleus.

The individual facts are known: the average length of the drunkard steps, the relative probability that a collision will be with an oxygen or hydrogen nucleus, the likelihood that the neutron will be absorbed or that it will bounce off the tank.

If we begin by considering a slow-moving neutron that collides with a hydrogen nucleus we may be able to say from earlier experiments that the chances are 99 to 1 that the neutron will bounce off. But what will this particular one do? It will *probably* bounce, but it *may* be absorbed. We decide the answer by spinning a roulette wheel that has, in place of the usual scheme of colors and numbers, just one hundred compartments. One of these is marked "bounce" and the other 99 are marked "absorbed."

If "absorbed" comes up, that's the end of this piece of history and we proceed to the next neutron.

Otherwise we spin another wheel to decide what the neutron's new direction will be and how much energy has been lost in the crash. Then we spin another wheel, set up for the proper odds, to tell us how long the next drunken step will be and with what sort of collision it will end.

One after another, we follow the careers of electrons. We pursue each until it is absorbed, loses so much of its energy that it is no longer of significance, or escapes from the tank to menace whoever stands in its way. By doing this for a large enough number of electrons we can get as precise a picture as we require of how many neutrons will escape. In one actual problem it was necessary to trace 10,000 of them through a million and a half collisions.

Done with actual roulette wheels, this would have been the work of several busy years, at the conclusion of which the information would have been so tardy as to be useless. An electronic calculator performed the equivalent of those million-odd wheel spins in three hours.

As with the dice questions of de Méré and Pascal, the roulette speculations of Ulam and von Neumann are spreading usefully to other fields. Monte Carlo method has been used in analyzing ground-controlled-approach systems for landing aircraft. It seems to be especially useful in the aerodynamic problems that arise as aircraft reach high altitudes where the air is so thin that the molecules may be yards apart. Individual collisions between craft and molecules become tremendously important, and it is no longer possible to regard the air as continuous. An approach through probability, as by Monte Carlo method, is needed.

Daniel D. McCracken, who worked on the Los Alamos project called Monte Carlo, visualizes all sorts of applications in quite different fields. He suggests telephone-exchange operation, traffic control, department-store inventories. But for many complex problems, he warns, better electronic calculators than any now in existence will be needed. They'll have to be able to solve problems requiring hundreds of millions of trials.

Meanwhile, the electronic-roulette-wheel method can be used on such ordinary problems as how to schedule work in a cabinet shop. Information is assembled first: tools are a drill press, table saw, lathe; three men are employed. Time for each operation is learned, including the fact that for one job it may vary from twelve to fifteen minutes as the worker becomes tired or bored.

An efficient schedule might be arrived at over some weeks or months by trial and observation. But electronic tracing of all the probability sequences could give a quick answer, and with greater assurance that it is the best.

Shielding for safety is not the only phase of atom-bomb craft in which the part played by probability must be recognized. Between the Spanish Civil War and World War II, before "bomb" meant what it does now, J. B. S. Haldane produced a bitter little study of air-raid protection that cuts even more deeply today. He began by dismissing minor risks: "Incendiaries have proved a negligible danger to life in Spain, and gas is also negligible except for babies and those whose respirators do not fit."

He then went on to show how dispersal may increase the value of p (standing in his formula for the probability of a specified death) "as when a child is evacuated from a fairly solid house into a flimsy hut. It merely insures that no single bomb will kill a large number of people, while increasing the probability that a single bomb will kill at least one. . . . The argument that a number of people must not be concentrated in one place in order that a single bomb should not kill hundreds is clearly fallacious when applied to a war in which the total casualties will be large. It is, however, true that a small group of key men each of whom can replace another should not be grouped together."

There is also the point of view of the taxi driver at Los Alamos, in Dexter Masters' novel *The Accident:* "But then I was reading in the paper just the other day about one of them saying there wasn't more than one chance in God-knows-what, a trillion maybe, that these Bikini bombs could blow up the world. I said to myself, this seems pretty safe odds. But then I said to myself, hey! how come any odds at all? Who's running this show anyway? I sort of get to wondering every once in a while whether anybody knows the middle and end of what's going on as well as the beginning."

CHAPTER 6

The Strategy of Winning

*Beyond chance; speculation;
why the rich get richer;
and the theory of games.*

You MAY recall wily Joe, the neighbor who tried to take money off you back in the first chapter. The trap he set was an offer to you to bet one to two on what looked like sure-enough two-to-one odds but actually were three to one.

Joe picked up that scheme from an eighteenth-century mathematician, but now he has been hearing about the work of a couple of his own contemporaries, John von Neumann, a mathematician, and Oskar Morgenstern, an economist. This work, generally known as the theory of games, is a way of analyzing competitive situations and evaluating and choosing possible strategies to fit them.

It appears that good old Joe now has a new proposal to make. Like the other one, its purpose is to lighten your coin pocket. Unlike the other one, however, it cannot be analyzed or solved by probability theory alone. Strategy has entered the picture, and analysis of Joe's new trap requires application of games theory.

The problem is deceptively simple. It is given the technical description of "two-strategy, 2×2 game" by J. D. Williams [*] of the Rand Corporation, an organization of scientists that has been conducting research for the U. S. Air Force aimed at the application of games theory to war.

Says Joe then: "It's a good night for matching pennies —too hot for anything more strenuous. In fact, it's pretty warm to flip actual coins, so let's just lean back and *say* 'heads' or 'tails' instead."

"All right so far," you agree.

"And to put a little variety into the game," Joe goes on, "I'll give you $3 when I call tails and you call heads. I'll give you $1 when it is the other way around. And when we match you give me $2 to make it even."

At this point you do a little figuring. On the basis of pure chance, which would apply if this were actual coin-tossing, the offer is fair enough. In the long run, out of each four tosses you would win $3 once and $1 once and lose $2 twice, for an even break.

But here the call is at the choice of the players. Strategy comes into it; and so does the theory of games, which is

<hr/>

[*] See Mr. Williams' *The Compleat Strategyst*, McGraw-Hill, 1954; and for some more on games theory, "Strategy in Poker, Business & War," by John McDonald, Norton, 1950.

a way of choosing a strategy.

As Joe looks at the strategical problem, his better call is heads because that costs him only one-third as much as tails when not matched and wins the same amount as tails when matched. If you make your calls at random, as if you really were flipping a coin, Joe need only stick to calling heads in order to win $2 on half the tosses and lose $1 on the others, for an easy profit of 50¢ a toss over the long run.

As you see it, your better choice also is heads—if Joe is making his choices at random. Half the time you'll match Joe's call of heads and lose $2. The other half of the time Joe will call tails and owe you $3. You'll average 50¢ profit per toss.

That's fine, but . . .

As soon as you find that Joe is not following a random pattern you will instantly depart from your all-heads strategy, because against Joe's use of the same call you are losing steadily.

Now Joe must change his plan too, or lose his shirt.

You are both arriving at the point assumed by the theory of games, that of full understanding of the strategy of the other.

Assuming Joe has his wits about him (and we already know he is pretty acute when your money is involved) he is bound in the end to adopt that strategy which will do the most for him against the best strategy you can adopt against it. And it is up to you to adopt the plan that will give you the biggest gain or the smallest loss against Joe's best response.

The methods of games theory have been used to discover, and prove, that your best strategy in this instance is to call heads and tails in a ratio of three to five. Of course you must mix up these calls in a random fashion so that all Joe can know about any single call is its probability: 3 in 8 it's heads. The random order you want is what you would get if, for instance, you put into a hat three slips of paper marked heads and five marked tails, stirred them up, drew one; then put it back before making the next draw; and so on.

By this strategy you will lose an average of $1 for each eight flips, but it is still your best strategy. By any other you will lose more against an opponent who is using *his* best strategy.

Which proves that this game, a fair one when played by chance, is an unfair game when free choice of strategy is allowed. Your best move, when it comes right down to it, is to put your fist firmly into your money pocket and hurry home.

Another thing that games theorists, including those who are off on their own hook rather than following von Neumann, have learned is just as discouraging to most of us: in carefully controlled model games the rich tend to get richer and the poor to get poorer. This fact, no surprise to pessimistic observers of life, seems to follow from at least two causes, one of which has to do with chance and the other with strategy.

The man who enters a contest with modest capital can

be wiped out by a series of bad breaks. Such a run is likely. It has a predictable probability, as you will see in the puzzles at the back of the book. If the unfavorable run hits him before a favorable one has augmented his capital sufficiently, he's done for, and this is a sequence just as probable as the opposite situation.

The man of wealth can ride out a bad run if it doesn't go on too long, and he can do so even if he has not had a lucky streak first. So he has a chance of going on to become an eventual winner even if he starts badly.

It is worth noting, though, that the advantage of wealth is important only where odds are even or favorable or where the game—whether academic model, Las Vegas roulette, or merging railroads—is a short-run proposition. In the long run a gamble against even slightly unfair odds will lose, no matter what the capital position of the unwary speculator.

The second reason for the poor man's poor outlook is that his strategy is more likely to be bad. Model games observed and analyzed at the University of Washington have shown a tendency for the poor to take reckless and extravagant gambles, increasing the probability of their losing all they have.

It's not hard to believe that things demonstrated in model games and mathematical theories derived from them have a real connection with economic life. Business analysts have long agreed, for instance, that a leading cause of failure of new businesses is inadequate capital.

The old finger game is another that von Neumann ana-

HOW TO WIN AT MORRA

		YOU	ENEMY
"three"	"two"	0	0
three	two	0	0
two	one	4	0
three (no score)	one	0	0
two	three	4	0
one	three	0	5
one	one	0	0
two	one	0	0
two	two	0	5
one	two	0	0
three	three	4	0
three	three	4	0
		16	10

lyzed. This is the one in which two players simultaneously show one, two, or three fingers and at the same time each calls out what he thinks his enemy is showing. There is no payoff if both guess right or both guess wrong. But if one player guesses right, the other pays him as many pennies (or dollars or matches) as the total number of fingers extended by the two players.

The strategy that von Neumann worked out mathematically for this ancient game (which has sometimes been called Morra) will usually win, should at least break even.

"three"   "two"   "one"

Do this 5 out of 12 plays ..... This 4 out of 12 .... and this 3 out of 12.

You are instructed to keep guessing four as the combined number of fingers; and out of each 12 games to show one finger 5 times, two fingers 4 times, three fingers 3 times. Keep the order well-mixed, of course, as nearly random as you can manage, or your opponent will solve your order of numbers and beat you. In making your calls, of course, you mentally subtract from four the number of fingers you are about to show, and name the difference.

The purpose of games theory is to study strategy. Its frivolous application is to games, such as poker. Its most serious potential application is to economics—the behavior of men in the marketplace, the strategies of buying and selling, of combinations and monopolies, of speculation and investment.

To get at the strategies underlying these things and others, von Neumann invented a game that is simple enough to study in detail, just complex enough to represent the necessary elements. It is a primitive form of straight poker, no draw, all cards face down. For his purposes he limits it to two players and two possible bets, low and high.

Using his simple model, von Neumann has been able to prove mathematically such bases of strategy as we have been talking about. One is that the best strategy, in general, is based on the assumption that whatever strategy you adopt will be found out by your opponent; and since he has found you out and acted on what he has found, you had best accept the highest gain that is possible against his best policy. In the long run you will lose by gambling for more.

Applied to a real game of poker under actual conditions, this establishes the need for bluffing and makes it profitable in the end to bluff even though you lose on some of your bluffs.

For bluffing is a kind of randomizing. If you never bluff, you establish a direct and all-too-apparent relationship between your bet and the value of your hand. You'll never lose much on your poor hands, it is true. But you'll never win much on your good ones because your betting on them will be a dead giveaway, and no one that you can beat will bet against you. Bluffing thus becomes as im-

portant for long-range strategy as for the possible immediate gain, and it need not be immediately successful to be gainful.

Growing out of this is the necessity to prevent your opponent from doing too well with a similar strategy. Thus you must occasionally call his bets while yourself holding mediocre cards, in order to catch him bluffing and make it excessively costly for him to bluff too frequently.

Of all immediate applications of games theory, it appears that the most urgent is to military strategy—"appears" because the very question as to whether games theory is being put to practical use in offensive and defensive war planning is itself a military secret.

It is apparent, however, that many of the problems of warfare can be studied through simplified models. They often turn out then to be forms of such games-theory models as the duel or the search.

The strategy of when to fire in a meeting of missile and anti-missile missile, for instance, is a real military question of the duel type. At bottom it is the same problem that has faced many a duelist in the quieter days of merely private violence.

You have one bullet. So has your opponent. You advance toward one another in the half-light of the traditional dueling hour. At the initial distance, and in the poor light, firing at once is obviously folly. If you shoot too soon and miss you will be unarmed and helpless; if too late, you will have been shot down before firing.

What is a simple problem when involving two marksmen of equal ability and equal arms becomes complex as new factors enter: differences in marksmanship; or differences in speed, when the duelists are airplanes, say; or when one side or the other is made up of more than one weapon; or where, as in usual practice, the gun contains more than a single bullet.

The theory of games has solved such questions for certain limited conditions. It cannot be said whether success has been achieved at the higher levels of military reality, but the degree of secrecy with which the subject has been draped indicates earnest and promising attempts, at the least.

For a final instance that ties games theory directly to probability, consider "The Final Problem," a Sherlock Holmes story that von Neumann and Morgenstern have used as a model.

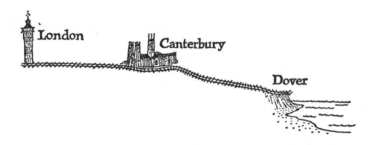

Holmes' ancient enemy Professor Moriarty is pursuing the great detective with murder in mind, and it is understood that if he succeeds in catching him Holmes must die. Holmes boards a train at London for Dover, from where he can flee to the Continent. Moriarty charters a train and follows close behind. There is only one stop before Dover—Canterbury.

Each must choose blindly, or by logic, where to leave the train.

If they choose the same station, Moriarty catches Holmes and thus is the winner.

But if Holmes gets off at Canterbury and Moriarty guesses wrong, the game could be called a draw, since Holmes will still not have made good his escape from England.

The classical approach to such a problem would call for an attempt to outreason the opponent, as in the childhood game of odd-or-even. ("He'll figure that I'll figure that . . . so I'll go one step further and . . .") Games theory, however, assumes—as well it might with such brilliant opponents as Holmes and the Professor—that each can carry the reasoning to the point of bafflement. What is needed, then, is an unforeseeable or random strategy.

For the computation a mathematical value must be assigned to the alternatives. Taking it from Moriarty's point of view, this might be 100 if he matches Holmes' choice—that is, catches him—but only minus 50 if he misses by going to Dover since in this case he may have another chance at Holmes.

On this basis, Holmes' best strategy is to randomize his choice on a basis that will make Canterbury a 60% probability. That is, he can drop into a hat ten slips of which six are marked "Canterbury" and four "Dover" and draw one.

Moriarty should decide similarly but make Dover the 60% probability.

The most likely occurrence then is Canterbury for Holmes and Dover for the Professor, which is precisely the outcome that Conan Doyle selects. This outcome, a draw for the antagonists, is only a 36% probability, however (60% × 60%, since these are the chances that each will make the decision in question).

The reverse may occur—Moriarty off at Canterbury, Holmes speeding on to Dover and safety—with a 16% probability (40% × 40%).

Or they may match, producing the end of Holmes, on a 48% probability. This is the sum of two 24% chances (60% × 40% for a Canterbury match, 40% × 60% for both hitting on Dover).

Note that the percentages add up to 100, as they must if our figuring is straight. There is, as in all probability calculations, exactly a 100% chance that one or another of the alternatives will occur.

Since the figures show Holmes as good as 48% dead from the beginning, he has reason to be thankful for a strategy that does in fact earn him a draw.

CHAPTER 7

Probability
Deals a Hand

Chance and 52 cards; bridge and poker
and the mathematics of doing better at them.

IF YOU play bridge you may have wondered about the rule that awards you 300 points for having scored one game in an uncompleted rubber. Like most of the rules of poker, and both the rules and the bidding systems of bridge, this is based on a more-or-less accurate calculation of probabilities. It might be interesting to see how close the bonus is to what you are entitled to on the basis of probability.

The rules provide that if you win a rubber by 2 games to 0 you get a bonus of 700. For winning 2 to 1, the bonus is 500.

Now let's see what your expectation is after you have won a single game. You have an even chance of winning the next one. Multiply this 1/2 probability by the 700 bonus you will receive and you get 350.

But there is also an equal likelihood that your opponents will win the second game, at which point each side will have an equal chance at a 500 bonus. The value of this expectation (a 1/4 chance at 500) is worth 125 points to each side. Since your expectation of 125 should be added to the 350, and your opponents' should be subtracted from it, you may as well regard these as canceling out.

So it seems that a first game is worth 350. Are the rules then mistaken in valuing it at only 300? Not entirely— because it is somewhat harder to make that second game than the first one; the winner of a game is in the position called vulnerable in which overbidding is subject to heavy penalties.

FOUR DIVISIONS OF MANKIND

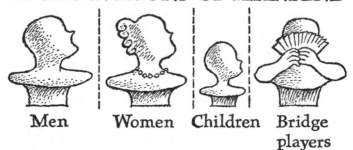

Men   Women   Children   Bridge
players

The last time I played bridge, two Yarboroughs were dealt in the course of some 25 deals of four hands, for a frequency of 1 in 50. Two such hands seemed to us rather excessive in one short evening, since a Yarborough is a collection containing nothing above a ten-spot.

How rare, we wondered, is such a hand?

Begin by calculating the chance that the first card you receive will be a ten or lower. Since 36 of the deck of 52 cards are poor enough to be at home in a Yarborough, the chance is 36/52.

Of the remaining 51 cards, 35 are tens or less, giving a 35/51 probability for the second. The chance with the third card then becomes 34/50. Continue this for 13 cards, multiply together the 13 fractions, and the result will be approximately 1/275. We had more than five times our share that evening, then.

This special name for a bad hand is said to go back to a Lord Yarborough, a whist player who was prepared to bet £1,000 to £1 against any given hand's being so bad that it contained no card above a nine-spot. This original Yarborough obviously would be harder to come by than the ten-spot-high hand to which the name has recently been extended. But how much harder? Would you be justified in risking a dollar for such a chance of winning a thousand?

The calculation is made in fashion similar to the other one, by multiplying together the 13 fractions of the series that begins with 32/52 and 31/51 and ends with 20/36. This gives 1/1,828. Yarborough's bet was a shrewd one, since it will win nearly twice as much money in the long run as it will lose.

In connection with the philosophy of chance and wagers, some things about the same bet from the other man's point of view are worth looking at. One is that it offers the same kind of long-chance bet (you'll probably lose, but not much, and if you should win you'd win a lot) that lotteries provide. Considering the pleasures of anticipation and hope, there may be times when one chance in 1,828 of winning a thousand dollars is worth the price of one dollar.

A very good hand is just as likely, or unlikely, as a very bad one; and the bridge-player's dream hand of 13 spades is not often seen. Such a hand is reported perhaps two dozen times a year in the United States.

Just what are the odds against your getting one on the next deal? The chance of getting 13 spades is, of course, exactly the same as of getting any other group of 13 cards, good or bad. Since there are 13 to a hand and 52 cards to a deck, the question we are asking is how many different 13-combinations are possible with 52 things. The calculation illustrates a method that can be applied to many other interesting problems.

The first card dealt to you may be any of the 13 spades without preventing you from getting the prize hand we are talking about. So your chance of starting out right is 13/52. Of the 51 remaining cards, 12 are spades, so your chance with the second card is 12/51. With the third it is 11/50, and so on down to the thirteenth when it is 1/40.

(Note at this point one side issue: even after receiving 12 spades in a row you are 40 times as likely to end with a hand containing 12 spades and one card of another suit as you are to get the perfect hand you're after.)

Multiply together these fractions according to the rule and you will find that the chance of the 13-spade hand is one in 635,013,559,600. Since there is an equal chance for each of the other suits, the probability of a one-suit hand is four times as good, or one chance in 158,753,389,900.

The bridge authority Oswald Jacoby once tried to square this figure with the frequency with which one-suit hands are reported in American newspapers. He estimated there might be 20 million players each dealing 30 hands a week. A likely expectation, then, would be one all-spade hand a year, or four or five one-suiters all told.

Why the greater number actually reported? And why is it nearly always spades? Practical joke, usually, suggests Jacoby. And I can remember being at a table at which all four players received one-suit hands, an occasion that just possibly would have gone down in local history if my kibitzing teen-age daughters, who had stacked the deck, had been able to choke back their giggles.

If we had done a little arithmetic—quite a little arithmetic—we might have become suspicious without the giggles. The chance against a deal in which *all four* players receive perfect hands is 28 digits to 1: 2 octillions, 235 septillions, and so on. Even in a world rather well-stocked with bridge players this could be expected to happen no oftener than once in a good many billion years.

Estimating probabilities enters a good deal more directly than all this into many of the circumstances of play. If declarer and partner hold the ace and king of a suit and the opponents have four including the queen, what is the chance that the queen will fall if ace and king are led?

There is a 936/2,300 chance that the cards will be divided two and two, in which case the queen will fall. There is an additional 1,244/2,300 chance that the division will be 3 and 1; and if it is, there is 1 chance in 4 that the lone card will be the queen, in which case also it will fall. Add the two-and-two chance to 1/4 of the three-and-one, and you will find the odds in favor of catching the queen to be 1.13 to 1. So it is a good rule, and generally observed, to lead ace and king when queen and three are in the opposing hands.

Another piece of information of interest to bridge players, though of no particular value to them, is how often a suit of a certain strength may be expected. How probable is it that your next hand will include at least one suit of four or more cards, among which are two of the top honors —ace, king, and queen? You can expect this fairly biddable suit about twice in every five hands; so you are not entitled to complain if you fail to get something so good as this as much as half the time.

In the matter of distribution of suits there are 39 distinct types of hand. Of these the most frequent is 4-4-3-2, with a probability of 21.55%. A singleton will occur in about one-fourth of all hands.

Both these figures come from an elaborate book on the mathematical theory of bridge, prepared with the aid of electric calculators by Emile Borel and André Chéron and published in France. It is on such calculations, more or less accurate and complete, that scientific systems of bidding and play depend.

Poker is a game of personalities and strategies, but the groundwork on which these must be built if they are to succeed is an understanding of probabilities. This is something every good poker player has, though he may have acquired his understanding at play rather than in study or calculation, and he may not be entirely aware that he has it.

The unidentified men who created poker, refining it as they went along, ranked the possible hands in value strictly in accordance with the probabilities, although flushes were somehow misplaced for a while. A ranking of hands naturally begins with a calculation of how many different hands are possible on a deal of five cards from the usual deck of 52. The figures are:

$$\frac{52 \times 51 \times 50 \times 49 \times 48}{5 \times 4 \times 3 \times 2 \times 1} = 2{,}598{,}960.$$

And, incidentally, if you use this method to work out other probabilities for yourself, don't overlook the time you can save by canceling.

Out of these 2,598,960 possible hands, 40 are straight flushes (four of them royal), 614 are four of a kind, and so on down. This translates into the table shown on the following page.

At least, this is a table that has been widely offered, though often with slight variations. In fact, it would be difficult to find two tables that agree, and many of the

FREQUENCY OF POKER HANDS

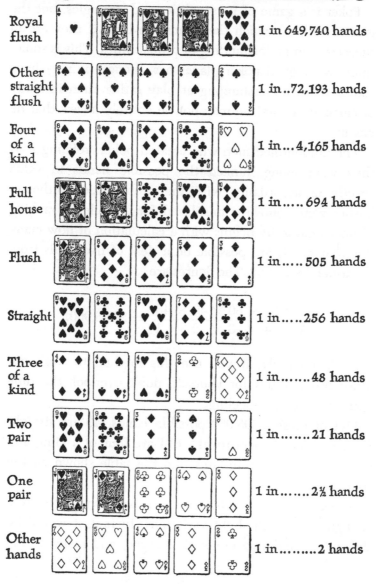

Royal flush	1 in 649,740 hands
Other straight flush	1 in ..72,193 hands
Four of a kind	1 in ...4,165 hands
Full house	1 in .....694 hands
Flush	1 in .....505 hands
Straight	1 in .....256 hands
Three of a kind	1 in ....48 hands
Two pair	1 in ....21 hands
One pair	1 in ....2½ hands
Other hands	1 in ....2 hands

much-used figures given by Hoyle can now be proved wildly incorrect.

It is no wonder he and others have had trouble. One of the simplest things to calculate is the probability of a flush, or so it seems. At least three authoritative writers agree with Hoyle that the chance is 1 in 509. The leading newspaper supplement *This Week* gives 1 in 508, possibly confused by the fact that a chance of 1 in 509 is odds of 508 to 1. George Gamov, who was an entertaining writer as well as a good scientist, figured 1 in 505. My own result, as it happens, agrees with his.

You might enjoy checking both the calculation and the logic. We may be wrong.

The first card can be anything—for a probability of 1/1.

The second can be any of the remaining 12 of the same suit as the first one, in a pack that is now down to 51. Probability of getting one of these: 12/51.

Similarly, for the remaining cards the chances are 11/50, 10/49, and 9/48. Multiply these fractions together and the result is 1/505.

There is one more thing to consider. The flush you get might possibly be a straight flush. But this possibility, including royal as well as other straight flushes, is only 1/64,974, which is not enough to change the figure or account for the disagreement.

For an example of the pitfalls awaiting the calculator of chances in more complex situations, take the case of the full house. In his fascinating and wide-ranging book *One Two Three . . . Infinity,* Gamov says the chance of a full house is the product of 6/50, 5/49, and 4/48, which is 1/980. It looks as if he started by saying the first card can be anything, which is true; and that the second card can also be any of those remaining, which is also true. But his series of fractions then assumes that the first two cards were of different denominations—not a pair of aces, say, or a pair of ten-spots, which they may have been. So several of the possibilities are cut off short after being allowed in the second step.

Actually there are ten possible arrangements leading to a full house, each of them having a probability of 3/20,825. This works out to 1 chance in 694, and that's what the table says.

All these things are interesting and possibly helpful in assessing the value of a hand. But the chances on the draw have a more immediate application to the strategies and decisions of actual play. Besides, they demonstrate some of the quick-and-simple calculations of chances.

Suppose you have been dealt a four-straight flush open at both ends; for instance, the five, six, seven, and eight of hearts plus another card of no value to your hand. What is your chance of improving your hand substantially if you discard the odd card and draw one?

There are four possible kinds of improved hand that you may achieve: a straight flush, a flush, a straight, or a pair.

The deck from which you will draw consists, as far as you are concerned, of 47 cards. This is true even though in fact it is much smaller, since your opponents have also been dealt cards from it. But, for all you can know at this moment, the one you draw may be any of the 47 that you haven't seen; and each one of them is just as likely as any other.

Since only two cards, the four and the nine of hearts, will complete your straight flush, you have just two chances in 47 of that happy event.

These are seven hearts other than those two and the four you hold. Drawing any one of these will give you an ordinary flush. The probability is 7 in 47.

The four or the nine of any of the other three suits would give you a straight—a 6/47 probability.

If you get any of the fives, sixes, sevens, or eights in the three suits in which you do not already hold these cards, you will at least have the consolation of a pair. The probability of this is 12/47.

Since any one of these possibilities will serve, the chance of improving your hand on this one-card draw is the sum of them, which is 27/47 or a little better than an even chance.

If you add up the first three fractions, without including the chance of a mere pair, you will find the probability of getting a really good hand when drawing to an open straight flush. It is very nearly 1 in 3, or 2 to 1 against you. Hoyle, by the way, gives the odds as 3 to 1. This is a substantial error; it could even cost you money.

Given three kings, or threes of any other kind, on the deal, what are your chances of turning them into four of a kind when you discard and draw two? Of the 47 cards you haven't seen, only one will do the trick. So you have a 1/47 probability of succeeding with the first card drawn, and a 46/47 likelihood of failing. Having failed, you will have a 1/46 chance with the second card. Multiplying together these two figures and adding them to the first, you get 2 chances in 47. Threes will not very often turn into fours.

Here is an interesting one: What does the fact that you yourself hold a pair or two pairs tell you about the probability that your opponent holds one also?

It might seem that your hand has used up one or two of the possible pairs in the deck, and so his chances are reduced. Actually it works the other way. Your holding pairs reduces the variety of the cards remaining and so slightly increases his chances. When you hold four of a kind you can figure the chances of any opponent holding a pair are about 10% stronger than when you hold nothing. (That's good; it may encourage him to stay in.)

For a look at the different ways in which a calculation can be made and at how much time one way can save over another, let's turn to the four flush. It's a hand that looks very encouraging but usually loses money for any holder who takes it seriously. Thus it produced the word used to describe a man whose packaging is better than his contents.

How likely are you to get one of these tempters on the deal?

Following the method we've been using, you will say that there are five ways to get such a hand, since the odd card can be the first, second, third, fourth, or fifth of those dealt to you.

Of these five, let's first take the one in which the useless card is the last one. You might note this sequence as FFFFx, with F standing for whatever suit the near-flush turns out to be, and x for any card of any other suit.

The first card can be anything without affecting the chances, so its probability is 52/52 or 1/1.

To get the sequence given above, the next card must be of the same suit as the first, of which the chance is now 12/51. In the same way, for the next two cards you'll find probabilities of 11/50 and 10/49. There are now 48 cards left, and 39 of them are in a suit other than that of your four cards. You must draw one of them now or you'll spoil your four flush by making it into a real one. Multiply the other fractions by each other and by 39/48 and you'll get 143/3332.

If you go through the other four possible cases (FFFxF, FFxFF, and so on) you'll find the same probability for each of them, as you might well expect. Five times the probability of the one case comes to about 1 in 23—your chance of receiving a four flush on any given deal.

The quicker way to get at this is worth a good look, since it illustrates the general method of calculating what are called combinations.

If you look back to page 106 you will see the setup for figuring out the number of possible poker hands. This might be called the number of ways that 52 different things can be formed into groups of 5.

You can see that you form the lower part of the expression by multiplying the size of the group by each smaller number that exists, all the way to 1. And you form the upper part by multiplying the number of things by each smaller number until you have as many numbers above the line as below.

This is a clumsy explanation. But if you will look at the arrangement just mentioned you will get the idea. And here it is for the case at hand, the number of ways that the 13 spades can be formed into groups of 4:

$$\frac{13 \times 12 \times 11 \times 10}{4 \times\ \ 3 \times\ \ 2 \times\ \ 1}$$

But since any of the 39 cards that are not spades will do for the fifth member of this hand, you must multiply the expression above by 39. And you must multiply again by 4, since spades is only one of the four suits in which you might get an almost-flush. Some canceling and a little arithmetic will tell you that we have found the number of ways a four flush may be dealt to be 111,540. Divide the number of possible poker hands (already shown to be 2,598,960) by this, and you'll verify the more cumbersome calculation that a four flush will be dealt once in each 23 hands—approximately, and in the long run.

Whew.

CHAPTER 8

How to Look at a Statistic

*What are the chances that an opinion poll,
a medical report, or an accident warning
means what it seems to say?*

LET'S SAY you're in the business of making automobile
tires. Tests on a type you've been making tell you it is
good, on the average, for 20,000 miles. They tell you,
further, that of every six tires you turn out, one will last
less than 18,400 miles and one will run more than 21,600.
The other two-thirds of your merchandise will fall some-
where between in durability.

You know this because you have a quality-control department engaged in applying statistical method, which is
in the main a use of probability theory.

Now comes your laboratory chief to tell you that a new
rubber formula produces what seems to be a more durable

tire. A sample of 64 has been run to destruction, showing a mean average life of 20,400 miles.

Is the new tire really better than the old? Or is the apparent improvement just a matter of chance, a lucky sample?

Your statistician will explain it all to you, probably in somewhat patronizing tones. What it will all come down to is that, by probability theory, there is 1 chance in 20 that a difference this size could be an accident. You can proceed with a changeover to the new rubber, having a reasonable certainty (19 to 1) that the new stuff actually is better than the old.

Sampling is one of our most useful techniques for studying a multitude of things. Polls sample public opinion because it would be hopelessly expensive to ask questions of the whole population. A manufacturer tests a sample of the light bulbs he makes to find out how long they will burn; if instead he tested them all, what would he have left to sell? An editor samples a manuscript because there are only so many hours in a day. And besides: "You don't have to eat all of an egg to know if it is bad."

In those words lies the basis of the theory of sampling. We can learn a little about the process by watching the editor at work. He reads a few lines here and a few there —large enough in number to get him an adequate sample, varied enough to protect him against a writer whose skill improves after a bad opening scene. The less consistent the writer is and the more uneven his style, the more of the manuscript the editor will have to read to obtain a fair idea of its average quality.

So it is in scientific sampling. When you read of a conclusion that arises from sampling, as do a great many of the things you read or hear about these days, ask yourself two things. Is it a fair sample? Is it big enough?

This reminds Irving Geis, the man behind all these pictures, of a scene in a Chaplin movie: A customer offers his watch for a loan. Chaplin as pawnbroker examines the watch, knocks off the back, unscrews some innards, keeps on till the watch is completely dismembered. Then he hands the pieces back to the customer, shrugging his shoulders, refusing the loan.

Here, to sharpen your teeth on, are the first couple of paragraphs of a story carried in the *New York Times* under the head, "DOCTORS REPORTED FOR SECURITY PLAN."

"A recent poll in New Jersey indicates that most of the country's doctors would like to come under the Social Security old age and survivors insurance program, according to Representative Robert W. Kean, Republican of New Jersey.

"He announced today that the poll, conducted by the Essex County Medical Society, showed that New Jersey physicians favored inclusion by a 6-to-1 margin."

As you take a closer look at this poll and the facts behind the conclusion you will see how little it justifies any conclusion about "most of the country's doctors." Someone has assumed that Essex County accurately represents the nation as a whole. It may, but then again it may not. Essex County doctors may not even be typical of their New Jersey colleagues.

On top of that, as you would learn if you read the rest of the *Times* story, the 6-to-1 refers only to those doctors who returned a questionnaire postcard. Some 78% did not answer. Isn't there good reason to suspect that those in favor of the idea would be more inclined to mark a card and drop it into a mailbox than those who were opposed or indifferent?

For final consideration, here is a relevant fact that was omitted from the newspaper story. The questionnaire reached the physicians in an issue of the Bulletin of the Essex County Medical Society that contained, by no coincidence, an article by Congressman Kean arguing that Social Security should be extended to doctors.

We started with information from which it seemed we might reasonably draw this conclusion as to the probability: it is 6-to-1 that the next doctor you meet will favor extending Social Security to the medical profession. But in the end we find we can make this conclusion only about quite a special group. They can be realistically described not as U. S. doctors in general but merely as "the 22% of Essex County, N. J., doctors who replied to a questionnaire accompanying an article favoring one side of this controversial subject."

one of the Essex county N.J. doctors who filled out a biased questionnaire favoring a one-sided controversial subject— BUT couldn't find a stamp.

That's a sample of how far you can be misled by a sample cut on the bias.

But even knowing a sample is unbiased is not sufficient. You must also be sure it is big enough. The adequacy of the size of a sample can be measured only in terms of chance, a word that comes into statistical discussions at all points.

The probability that a figure from a sampling study is true for the whole group from which the sample was selected is given as the degree of significance. This may refer to whether the figure is accurate within a given number of dollars or tons or hours or people. Or to whether what appears to be the greater of two quantities really is the greater.

When the Bureau of the Census tells you that its sampling reveals the average (median) income of American families to be $3,500, it will also tell you how far to trust this figure. To the report will be added some such information as that the chances are 19 out of 20 that the average is correct within a hundred-dollar range each way.

This 5% level of significance is good enough for some purposes. For much scientific work the required level is 1%, which means the odds are 99 to 1 that the apparent difference, or whatever, is a true one. Something as probable as this is often described as "practically certain."

You may also meet this important concept in the shape of what is called a probable error. Take an intelligence test and you may learn (if you can pry this secret data away from the psychometrician) that your I.Q. is 133. This means you're pretty bright, probably.

It also means your intelligence has been sampled rather than fully measured. Even a relatively good test like the Stanford-Binet requires only a few hours and obviously samples only a tiny part of the most limited intellect, even within the area of talent that it covers. Its makers have concluded that it has a probable error of about 3%. Since 3% of 133 is about 4, your level would be expressed as 133 ± 4.

This is an expression meaning that if you were to take a

large number of tests exactly equal to this one, it's an even bet that your average score on them would come out within 4 points of 133, one way or the other. It means there is 1 chance in 4 that your I.Q. would turn out to be above 137. Dismally, it follows that the probability is also 1 in 4 that repeated testing would show your honest level to be below 129.

A probable-error table would enable you to figure out some more things. It would tell you that odds against a deviation of more than three probable errors either way are 21 to 1 against your really belonging to the below-113 intellectual set.

You can see why it is folly to regard such tests as precision instruments. Given two youngsters, a boy with an I.Q. rating of 125 and a girl with 133, what can you say about them? On the odds, there is 1 chance in 4 that the boy's true level is below 121. There is 1 chance in 4 that the girl's is above 137, as we have seen. So there is 1 chance in 16 that the girl stands at least 16 points higher than the boy. But the chance is equally good that he is just as clever as she is.

So it is with studies of magazine readership and advertising. If no figures estimating error or significance are to be found, better give the whole thing a big glassy stare. If they are there, take them to heart. You may avoid learning a remarkable lot that is not so.

Instead of the probable error you are likely to find something else, called the standard deviation or the standard error. It works much the same way but happens to be a good deal handier for mathematicians to work with. The difference is, one standard deviation each way will bracket almost exactly two-thirds of the cases instead of precisely one-half.

This part of statistics goes back, as a number of other useful ideas do, to Karl Gauss, the "prince of mathematicians," and his law of error. You won't be astounded to hear that it was derived from the theory of probability.

Suppose you clamp a rifle in a vise and fire thousands of rounds through it at a distant target that is just a big piece of cardboard. The bullets will not all go through the same hole, because arms and ammunition and air currents are not consistent. Instead they will form a pattern that seems at first to be highly irregular but which soon begins to take on form. There will be a heavy concentration of bullet holes, slowly fading off into a scattered few as the distance from its center increases.

The most remarkable thing about this pattern is how much you can predict about it without being anywhere in the vicinity or even knowing much of anything about firearms.

Fit a target-like series of concentric rings to the pattern. Make the center circle just big enough to take in one-half of the bullet holes. Draw the other circles so that each is the same distance from the next smaller one as the first is from the center point. Call the bullseye 10, the ring next to it 9, and so on.

Now here is what can be predicted through a knowledge of probabilities and nothing else: 7 out of each 22 bullet holes will be in the 9 ring, and 3 out of each 22 will be in the 8 ring. One in 26 will be in the next ring. The fraction will continue to shrink, reaching 2 in a million by the 4 ring.

Since these are probabilities, you can be practically certain that your predicted percentage will be very close to right for the rings that contain a large number of hits. Not so for the sparsely pinked outer rings; guessing them is like predicting the results of a mere handful of coin tosses.

Another thing you could do is chart the distribution of the bullet holes. First you'd draw a vertical bar of a height determined by the number of holes striking within one inch, let's say, of the center of the group. To the left, place another bar of a height proportional to the number of holes to be found between one and two inches away from the center in the left-hand half of the target. Continue this procedure to the left, and then do it to the right also.

Connect the centers of the tops of the bars and you'll have a sweeping curve.

No matter what kind of rifle you've used or how far from the target it was, you'll get the same bell-shaped curve.

Graph the distribution of the heights of American men, and oddly enough you'll get just about exactly the same curve again. It will be high in the center, because there are more men of 5 feet 8 inches (or maybe the average is up an inch by now, but never mind) than any other height. The number who are 5'7" is slightly smaller, and so is the number who are 5'9". Shorter bars on either side of these three will represent the 5'6" group and the 5'10". And so on. By the time you pass 5 feet in one direction and 6 feet 4 in the other, the bars will be pretty tiny.

If you were to ask quite a large number of people to heft a box and estimate its weight to the nearest ounce, their guesses would follow this same curve rather closely. If the greatest number should guess 22 ounces, there will probably be almost—but not quite—as many guesses of 21 and of 23 ounces, somewhat fewer of 20 and of 24, and so on.

Will the big bulge come at the right weight? Maybe, maybe not. The most popular guess will probably be close to right, but people can be wrong in the mass just as they can individually, and a box of one size or shape will be quite consistently guessed heavier than one of different appearance and same weight. As noted in Chapter 3, an optimist named Condorcet discovered quite a time ago, to his final disillusionment, that individual errors do not al-

CHEST MEASUREMENTS OF SCOTTISH SOLDIERS

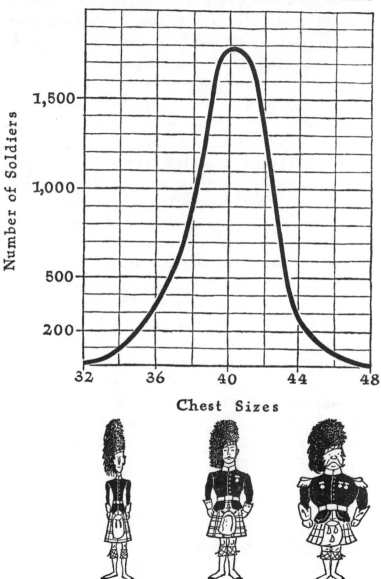

Chest Sizes

ways cancel each other out.

The chest measurements of Scottish soldiers have been shown to fit this same curve. So have the runs of a color or number on a roulette wheel, the velocities of molecules in a gas, and quite a lot of other things.

This fact so impressed many scientists and mathematicians in the days right after Gauss that they believed the normal curve to represent the nature of just about everything. They tried to force their data to fit it.

In fact, although it is remarkable how many and diverse things do fit this pattern, it is important to remember that there are many more distributions that do not. Human heights do, but human weights do not; nor do incomes. These two, by the way, form skew curves—the kind having one slope far steeper than the other. It's obvious that in a neighborhood where the mean (arithmetic average) income is $5,000 hardly any families will have incomes more than $3,000 under the average but a good many will receive in excess of $3,000 more than this average; and there will likely be a few with incomes many times the average.

This skewed or asymmetrical distribution produces a sad condition: most of us have below-average incomes.

An average than which most of the constituent figures are less is likely to be rather misleading. That's precisely why the ordinary arithmetic average has been abandoned for most statistical work with incomes. Used instead is the kind of average called a median, which is simply the figure that divides the whole distribution into two equal parts.

With a median, anyway, half of us can be above average.

CHAPTER **9**

The Great ESP Mystery

What happens when probability proves some of the most improbable things.

IT WAS perhaps inevitable that one of the great mysteries of the ages should eventually be tackled by means of probability theory and the statistical methods based on it.

Mind-reading and fortune-telling and all the other weird and wonderful experiences that make up what we call extrasensory perception are as old as history. Millions of people have believed them real, and just as many others have laughed them down as superstition.

The pursuit of this mystery begins with the kind of experience thousands of people—you yourself, perhaps— have had. This one is among many collected and investigated by the American Society for Psychical Research.

A teacher in Dallas, lying awake—or so he believes—one spring night, heard the rattle of a door. By the light from a street lamp he saw his father standing in the doorway. Since the father lived in California, his son thought for a moment that this was a surprise visit. But the father advanced silently across the room, shook his son's hand, and vanished.

Within seconds, a messenger appeared at the door and delivered a telegram. It reported the death of the father in Los Angeles earlier that evening.

The teacher recounted the vision to his wife, who by then had awakened. He described in detail his father's costume, including work clothes containing a pocket ruler —not things the older man would ordinarily have worn or carried.

On a later visit to California the son was shown the clothes his father had worn on the day he died, and they corresponded in every detail to those of the apparition.

Convinced psychical researchers might describe this as a case of telepathy. The father, in dying, had projected a powerful image of himself. The son had received it unconsciously and it had emerged into his conscious mind as he lay quietly in bed.

The alternate explanation is simply: coincidence.

The argument is that millions of people have dreams each night, a total of hundreds of billions of dreams each year. By chance alone a few out of this vast number should bear a startling resemblance to truth. Those few are the ones we hear about.

The most eminent of all workers with ESP is Dr. J. B. Rhine, of Duke University. His approach was to agree that either explanation is possible, and to view these spontaneous cases as merely suggestive.

What we must do, said Dr. Rhine quite a few years ago now, is set up controlled laboratory experiments. Then we can apply established statistical methods to tell us whether any results we get are real or a product of chance.

After considerable experimenting, Dr. Rhine and his colleagues evolved a method using a special deck of 25 cards containing five of each of these five types: cross, star, square, circle, wave.

These cards can be used to test for the existence of many different kinds of extrasensory perception. Perhaps the simplest is telepathy, or mind-reading. The experimenter sits behind a screen and takes cards one at a time from a shuffled pack. He lists each as he looks at it. At the same time the subject lists the card he thinks the experimenter has drawn.

The search for precognition—knowing things before they happen, as in fortune-telling—calls for only a slight change in procedure. The subject writes down the name of the card just *before* the experimenter shuffles the deck and draws one.

Clairvoyance is the ability to see or know things that have happened but are out of view. To rule out the possibility of mind-reading, an experiment in clairvoyance requires a situation in which the facts are not known to anyone anywhere.

One of the Duke experiments in clairvoyance shows how this is arranged, and it also is a good sample of the many other experiments in ESP that have been performed. It will also show how the validity of probability theory has been brought into question by the very fact that it seems to confirm the reality of ESP.

A scientist, Dr. Gaither Pratt, has met a person who seems from earlier experiments to have a high degree of extrasensory perception. The scientist and the subject synchronize their watches. They go into rooms in separate buildings on the Duke campus.

At the agreed-upon instant the experimenter begins to deal cards from a well-shuffled pack at a rate of one each minute. But he does not look at the cards. Only after he has gone through the whole deck does he turn it over and look at it or let anyone else do so. Then he copies on a piece of paper the order in which the cards lie.

Meanwhile, hundreds of yards away and out of view, the subject has been writing down his guesses about those cards at the same rate of one a minute.

After a run of 1,850 guesses, at a rate of 50 a day, the

two lists are checked by witnesses. It turns out the subject has guessed right 558 times.

Since there were five possibilities for each card, the subject should have hit the right one just about one-fifth of the time by sheer chance—for a total of 370. But how remarkable is it that he did so much better?

The established statistical methods used in other scientific work say that so good a result would occur by accident of lucky guessing only once in about 10 thousand billion billion times.

That number is 1 followed by 22 zeros. We can save space and energy by writing it 10^{22}.

Yet this actually happened. And there have been many other similar experiments showing an equally high degree of statistical significance.

Here is one of them. Mathematically it is only slightly less remarkable, and the probabilities are much easier to understand. You'll find the calculation quite familiar.

One day Dr. Rhine ran through the pack with a student named Hubert E. Pearce, Jr., who had a long record of successes. On this occasion Pearce called every one of the 25 correctly.

Could that be luck? What are the chances?

That depends on how the calling was done. If each card was replaced and the deck shuffled before the next call, it's easy to figure. You can see that since there were five kinds of cards in the deck, Pearce had one chance in five of calling the first one right and the same on the second. So his chance of calling *both* correctly by luck was one in

5×5 or 25.

You can verify this by listing the five possible guesses he could have made for the first card, then adding to each of these each of the five guesses he could have made for the second. The total will be 25 sequences, and only one of these could be right.

To find the chance that Pearce could be so lucky 25 times in a row, multiply 25 5's together. You'll find that his chance was one in 298,023,223,876,953,125. Quite likely, though, the calling was done by going through the pack and not replacing the cards. You can see that this will shorten the odds a bit. The first card will be as hard to guess as in the other arrangement—five chances in 25— but the last one will be a sure thing.

Then the probability will be one chance in the number given in this recent newspaper article. And the odds will be 1 to this same number minus 1, the newspaper figure being wrong to that extent.

Confusing the chance of something with the odds against it is a common error, by the way, and already touched on in the material on poker hands. But it's easy enough to keep the matter straight: if there is 1 chance in 4 of an occurrence, the odds are 3 to 1 against it.

But back to the case of the Welsh cousins. If the cards were called by going through the deck without replacement, we need the calculation for the number of different permutation of 25 things, five of each of five kinds. This is $25!$ divided by $(5!)^5$, which is a way of writing "factorial 25 divided by the fifth power of factorial 5."

Cousins in Britain Reported to Read Each Other's Minds

By the United Press

LONDON, March 17—The former president of the National Society for Psychical Research asserted here yesterday he had found two cousins who could read each other's minds.

Dr. Samuel Soal said 16-year-old Glyn Jones, of Capel Curig, Wales, correctly identified 25 picture cards "thought" at him by his cousin, Ieuan Jones, also 16.

"The odds against this happening by chance are 623,360,-473,125,120 to one," Dr. Soal said.

Dr. Soal described experiments with the cousins similar to those carried on at Duke University, in the United States. The two boys were separated, sometimes in different rooms, sometimes by screens, sometimes across a field and out of sight.

An impartial observer sat by each boy. Ieuan would watch Dr. Soal or an assistant turn over picture cards. He would concentrate on the picture but say nothing. At his separate post, Glyn, with another observer, would try to guess the picture cards in the correct order as they were revealed to Ieuan.

"The normal guesser would get only five right on the average, and could probably sit calling out cards all his life before he once fluked even 12 or 13 [correct guesses] out of the 25," Dr. Soal said.

However, Glyn often scored 23 or 24 correct guesses in the 25-card sequences, and hundreds of times picked 17 or 18 cards right, Dr. Soal said.

"I have never come across results like this," he said.

Dr. Soal said he has been experimenting with the two boys for about three years.

"Factorial" means merely the number in question multiplied by each digit smaller than itself. So first we must multiply 25 by 24, 23, and so on. Then we must multiply $5 \times 4 \times 3 \times 2 \times 1$ to get 120—and then multiply 120 by itself four times. The larger of these products divided by the smaller will give the long number that appears in the newspaper story.

The arithmetic is fairly prodigious, but the method is simple.

Figures like these from experiments like these seem to demonstrate the reality of telepathy, clairvoyance, precognition, and even telekinesis. In another of Dr. Soal's experiments the possibility of chance seemed to be about one in a number consisting of 2 followed by 35 zeros.

What, then, is the truth about ESP? Does it exist?

Scientists have offered three alternative explanations.

One is simply that it's all a mistake, a result of bad technique in either the experiments or the statistical analysis. But new experiments under different conditions answered the first criticism; in one of these the experimenter was in North Carolina and the subject in Zagreb, Jugoslavia. And the American Institute of Mathematical Statisticians has examined and approved the statistical work.

The second explanation is that it is all a fraud. Dr. George R. Price, research associate in the University of Minnesota's department of medicine, has suggested this. "I do not claim that I know how Soal cheated if he did cheat," says Price, "but . . ." And he goes on to tell how the experiments could be faked by use of two to four confederates. He ties down his argument with some words of Tom Paine's: ". . . is it more probable that nature should go out of her course, or that a man should tell a lie?"

Many scientists are unwilling to believe in either the dishonesty of their colleagues at Duke, London, Cambridge, and Harvard or in the reality of ESP. They necessarily attack the basis of the proof, which is the theory of probability. That's what turned a symposium on ESP in England recently into a critical discussion of the laws of chance, giving the question of ESP an importance beyond the phenomena themselves.

One thing that comes into this is the problem of randomizing, which runs all through probability and statistics. All sorts of ingenious tables and devices have been contrived in an effort to solve it, beginning with such early models as a pair of dice, a deck of cards, a roulette wheel.

The random is never quite random, it seems. G. Spencer Brown, a research lecturer at Oxford, points out one difficulty. This paradox appears in his book, *Probability and Scientific Inference* (Longmans, Green and Co., 1957).

We have a randomizing machine which produces a series of ones and noughts. We require for experimental purposes a random series of 16 ones and noughts. We start the machine which now gives us a series of 16 noughts. We of course reject this series as unsuitable and suspect the machine of being biased. It is returned to the makers for adjustment. When it comes back we have a very long experiment for which we require a random series of 2,000,000 ones and noughts. We leave the machine running all night, but on checking through the 2,000,000 ones and noughts it produces we are surprised to find not a single run of 16 noughts. Again we suspect it of being biased and send it back.

But what is its designer to say to all this? First we send it back because it produces 16 noughts in a row. Very well: he puts in a device to prevent its doing this. We then send it back because it never produces 16 noughts in a row. What is he to do now? First of all we use a specific criterion to reject the series the machine produces, and then we use the absence of this very criterion to reject another series it produces. It seems we are never satisfied.

Working with published tables of random numbers, Brown has gone on to show that by comparing one set of these numbers against another he can produce relationships of the same sort that are offered as evidence of ESP. He concludes that "any attempt to randomize, *of which tables of random numbers and psychical research experiments are both typical examples,* will lead all too frequently to the curious results which have been thought in the past by psychical researchers to be evidence of telepathy and whatnot."

Experimenters with ESP give themselves a rather large number of chances to succeed. A card-guessing experiment may show no more successes than chance could be expected to produce. It is then examined to see if perhaps the number of *failures* isn't significantly high. Nothing turning up there, the guesses are checked against the card that preceded or followed the one in question. A man can be pretty sure to hit a target if there are enough of them about.

Another randomizing failure is one that might be called corresponding patterns. This possibility is what would make it bad practice to inspect every tenth item, say, coming off an assembly line. If there were five, or ten, people producing one part of the finished thing, the inspector might be getting mostly their work. And the product of some single consistently fumble-fingered worker

could be largely overlooked.

This correspondence of patterns could occur in telepathy experiments too, perhaps somewhat in the manner of Sir Ronald Fisher's tea-tasting experiment: A lady, British of course, remarks that she can tell by taste whether the milk has been added to the tea or the tea to the milk. A skeptic presents her with four cups of tea of one sort and four of the other. She tastes, and identifies them all correctly.

What can this mean?

First, it may be that she really can tell tea and milk from milk and tea by taste.

Or, second, she may have made a series of lucky guesses, a one-chance-in-seventy long shot.* This is so unlikely that it would seem more reasonable to credit the lady's claims.

But wait. Perhaps the skeptic has arranged the cups in some simple pattern, probably without thinking about it . . . an alternation, perhaps. And the lady has chosen the same common pattern. This could greatly reduce the odds against a series of hits being made even if taste is no clue.

It is a possibility difficult or impossible to eliminate in many kinds of statistical work.

* Why these odds? For her first guess the lady has an even chance (1/2) however she guesses, since she knows there are four cups of each kind. On her second guess, she knows there remain three cups of this same kind and four of the other. By guessing the other she has a 4/7 chance of being right. Her third guess is an even chance again. The opposite choice will give her a 3/5 chance on the fourth trial. Fifth guess is an even chance. She has two chances in three on the sixth guess, an even guess on the seventh, and a sure thing on the eighth.

$$\frac{1}{2}\times\frac{4}{7}\times\frac{1}{2}\times\frac{3}{5}\times\frac{1}{2}\times\frac{2}{3}\times\frac{1}{2}\times\frac{1}{1}=\frac{1}{70}$$

CHAPTER 10

Living with Probabilities

Chance enters into life—
and death—
at a multitude of points;
the question is how to take it.

On trial for his life in the California courts a couple of years ago, Burton Abbott took pains to display conspicuously the jacket of a book he had met in one of his university courses. Neither the content of the book nor the fact that I wrote it is important at the moment, but the title *is* important: *How to Lie with Statistics.*

This was the silent reply of the defense to expert testimony about the clay in which a body was found buried and some mud scraped off Burton Abbott's boots. The question was one of pure probability: what is the likelihood that two samples of earth could be so similar by chance?

In another case two men died in San Quentin for the murder of a cab driver. According to Marshall Houts,* lawyer and former F.B.I. man, "the *only evidence* connecting them with the scene of the crime is the testimony of an expert witness that on the basis of *seven matching fiber transfers* between the clothing of the victim and the defendants, the probabilities are 1 in 1,280,000,000 that the defendants contacted the victim and his cab." (Mr. Houts evidently means to say that this is the claimed likelihood that chance rather than contact produced the series of similarities.)

The testimony was that seven bits of cloth fiber found clinging to the clothing of the accused men matched the clothing of the victim. Since the figure the witness gives is equal to the product of 20 taken seven times, it appears that the expert assigned a probability of 1 in 20 to each match.

But for real evidence of how badly a better understanding of chance is needed in courts of law, let's turn to a case in which the details of the reasoning are available.

On September 10, 1946, Police Officer Charles Odum died by gunshot wound. Joseph Trujillo was eventually put to death for the murder, and another man was given a life sentence.

A fiber match figured in this case too. The testimony was that since eleven matches were found, and there was only 1 chance in 10 that each could be an accidental re-

* *From Evidence to Proof*, Charles C. Thomas, Springfield, Ill., 1956.

semblance, the probability that chance produced the matches must be 1 in 100 billion.

But the key point of the case, as far as we are concerned, is the prosecution's argument that the bullet that killed the policeman came from a pistol belonging to Trujillo. The basis of this was a set of five matching characteristics:

1. Bullet and pistol were both 38 caliber; since there are at least six calibers, the chance of the two being the same would be no better than 1 in 5.

2. Rifling was right-hand in both cases; since it could be either right or left, this is 1 in 2.

3. Pistol and bullet both show five lands and grooves; the number might have been 4, 5, 6, 7, or 8 but "call it 4 to 1 to be conservative."

4. Both pistol and bullet showed chamber out of line with barrel. "This is a very unusual thing, but I think it would be safe to say it couldn't happen more than 1 time in 5."

5. "The bullet happened to be fired from a revolver, and this gun is a revolver, again one in two, because it might have been an automatic."

Multiplying these together the prosecutor arrived at odds of "one to 400, that this is the gun that was used in the killing of Officer Charles Odum that night."

As you can see, the weakness in all this convincing mathematics is that we don't know whether these are equally likely possibilities. As with d'Alembert's fallacy (see Chapter 1) this is fatal to the logic as surely as, along with the rest of the testimony, it was to the defendant.

In Point 1, is each caliber equally likely among firearms in general? Among pistols used by hold-up men in the area? A similar argument applies to each of the other points.

For all we know, criminals at the time and place in question may have strongly favored one particular model of weapon. Of all the pistols in underworld hands at the time, it may well be that one in five or ten would match the bullet to the extent indicated in the argument. And that is quite different from one in 400.

But this comes a little late, from Trujillo's point of view, anyway. So let's turn to some other fallacies in applying the rules of probability.

A fruit-grower once charged that his trees were being blighted by radio waves from a station close by. He went to work to prove his unlikely point: he put fence wire around some of his trees to shield them from the waves. Sure enough, and to the especial bafflement of agricultural experts, the shielded trees recovered miraculously while the rest of the orchard remained in blight. The probabilities clearly were millions to one against chance being the cause of the sudden improvement.

A somewhat similar ailment, a "little leaf" disease, began to increase among citrus trees. Fruit and foliage were stunted. Then it was found, in one Texas region, that a solution of iron sulphate would cure the ailment. In one grove after another, the treatment worked. But occasionally it failed, and it worked hardly at all when tried in Florida and California. Here again the situation was outside any reasonable probability.

When it was discovered that these ailments were produced by a deficiency in zinc in the soil, the whole story rapidly became clear. The radiophobic farmer's fence wire was galvanized; enough zinc washed off the wire to give the trees the tiny trace of zinc they needed. The iron sulphate did nothing for the other trees, but the zinc-coated buckets in which it was carried saved them. In regions where buckets other than galvanized were used, the trees went right on ailing.

There's a useful warning in these incidents. Note that probability led to the correct conclusion that the treatment was working, although it did not protect against an incorrect one as to why.

One of the momentary-miracle toothpastes advertised under big headlines: "NOT A SINGLE CAVITY IN OVER 2 YEARS." Testimony from ten users, all women for some reason, described about the same experience—cavities before, none after using.

NOT A SINGLE CAVITY IN 25 YEARS
(ADVT.)

Surely this proves something?

Well, let's see. Suppose you are in charge of research for a toothpaste-manufacturer or, for that matter, an advertising agency. You arrange with a couple of hundred women to switch to the dentifrice you're interested in. If your toothpaste is worthless, or anyway, no different from other toothpastes, it is not hard to predict what you will find after a two-year "test."

The results will follow fairly closely the normal curve. That is, a good number of ladies will have had about as many cavities as usual. A somewhat smaller number will have shown substantial improvement, and about as many will have had distinctly more cavities than in the earlier period. Quite a few will have suffered a shocking increase in dental decay . . . and a few will have had an enormous improvement.

If you are a lucky advertising man you will have enough perfect records in the last group to fill your layout. If you don't have enough, it's your own fault. You should have started with a larger group in order to increase the probability of winding up with ten winners.

All this doesn't prove the paste no good. As in cautious Scots courts, the verdict is "not proven."

Determining the merits of a drug or treatment is by no means simple, especially when the goal is information rather than testimonials. Any experimental technique less rigorous than the one known as "double blind" can give only questionable results in many of the most common situations, as we shall see.

There was a time when a drug was commonly tested by trying it on a few patients. If the patients did better than they had been doing, or said they did, it was regarded as a success. Then probability, which is to say the application of statistical treatment, came into things and demanded certain care in the choice of the sample.

But even a large sample can be wrong, as when a seasickness pill helped one group of sufferers and was hailed as a great discovery until in further experiments little sugar pills were found to be just as effective, at least on patients who were told they were receiving the new drug. It has turned out that as many as 40% of patients will respond to a sugar pill or other placebo in a manner indistinguishable from the effect of an active drug.

The ordinary controlled experiment having proved untrustworthy, experiments turned to a blind technique. No patient was told whether his pill was the drug or a placebo.

This was better, but false results still sometimes developed; because the doctor or nurse knew, and voice intonations were often enough to suggest to a patient whether he might or might not expect to benefit. And a doctor, knowing which patient was receiving the drug, might see improvement where it was not.

Today a well-conducted experiment uses two groups of patients, each alternately receiving drug and placebo. Neither patient nor physician may know which is which until a code is broken at the end of the experiment . . . *after* results of treatment have been judged, if it is that kind of experiment, by both patient and experimenters. When this "double blind" method is used, results can safely be assessed according to probabilities.

The language of probability is proving most useful in weather forecasting, since tomorrow's weather is never quite a sure thing. The atmosphere is a system following physical laws, but it is unstable and highly complex, and the observations of it on which forecasters rely are no more than a tiny sample. So it has become a common practice to make predictions in the form of "the chances of rain tomorrow are 7 in 10" or "70 percent." Compared with "rain probable," such a forecast is at the same time more precise and meaningful and considerably less pretentious.

Any sequence of weather, like any series at roulette or any bridge hand, is an improbability of a high order. Record lows are startling and so are record highs, even in New York City in August. Rapid fluctuations are unusual weather and so is a run of little change. Then, just to make it worse, a Princeton paleontologist comes out from behind his fossils with the news that although the weather has been getting warmer ever since the last glacial ice age we happen to be in a colder fluctuation at the moment—a moment he thinks will end along about 1965. Well, that's what it takes to make an unparalleled subject for conversation.

You might like to try a bit of long-range forecasting of your own, using the methods of probability. To predict good and bad days for next January, say, find out how many of each you had last January. Put a white marble in your hat for each good day, a black for each bad. Then start drawing marbles, predicting fair for New Year's Day if your first marble is white, and so on.

"You'll be hailed as a genius," says Thomas F. Malone,

NEW YORK'S WORST WEATHER

Record Temperatures for New York City 1871–1957

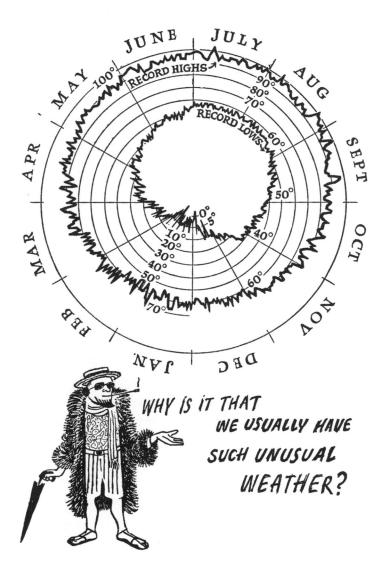

WHY IS IT THAT WE USUALLY HAVE SUCH UNUSUAL WEATHER?

secretary of the American Meteorological Society. "For short-range forecasts, people notice only your misses—but for long-range forecasts, all they notice is your hits."

Probability methods can answer some of the oddest questions, even political ones.

Senator A is going to win an election from Candidate B. As the election returns come in, what is the chance that the victorious Senator will lead all the way from the very beginning? You can find the answer by dividing the difference between the two candidates' votes by their sum.

Work it out for two and a half million votes to one and a half million. The difference (one million) divided by the sum (four million) gives one chance in four. Even with a landslide coming up, the Senator will probably have some bad moments if he puts much stock in the early returns.

Since Mendel, probability has been at the heart of genetics. An instance is found in color-blindness, which is fairly common in men, rare in women. Why? It appears to come from a defect in the sex chromosome called X. Female cells have two of these, males have one X and one Y. One perfect X-chromosome is enough.

So if on the average one X-chromosome in a hundred is defective, color-blindness will be found in one per cent of men. But in women color-blindness will occur only in the one case in 100 times 100 when both cells happen to be defective. And in observed fact, color-blindness does occur with about the frequency that this theorem of the multiplication of probabilities says it should.

Julian Huxley * has described the workings of chance through natural selection as "a mechanism for generating improbability of a very high order."

Says he: "Let us assume that the improbability of a favourable mutation extending, *without selection,* to all the individuals in a species is a million to one (a very low estimate, by the way). Then the improbability of two such favourable mutations both extending through the species is a billion [a British billion equals a U. S. trillion] to one. With ten separate mutations, the improbability becomes astronomical: yet we know that by artificial selection, man has been able to combine many times ten favourable mutations to produce the fowls or horses or wheats he wants.

"It is improbable in the highest degree that the human eye should have arisen 'by chance,' but with the aid of the machinery for producing improbabilities provided to life by Natural Selection, the improbability can be and has been actualized."

We can go back even further and consider the probability that life on earth might have begun spontaneously. A strong argument against this has been that, with a few tiny exceptions, all the organic material of which we have knowledge has been produced by other living organisms.

A recent experiment concentrated on one of these neglected exceptions. It duplicated conditions believed to have existed in the early days of our planet. A mixture of

* "Chance and Anti-Chance in Evolution," *The Fortnightly,* London, April 1946, Page 236.

water vapor, ammonia, methane, and hydrogen was circulated over an electric spark for a week. When the water was analyzed, amino acids were found . . . an exciting discovery to which consideration of probabilities brings significance.

Such a development could not be expected under natural conditions in a week. It would be highly improbable, but the experiment shows it is possible. It need only occur once.

Suppose such an event as happened in this seven-day experiment has only one chance in a thousand to occur in a year, 999 chances in a thousand of not happening. Multiply 999/1,000 together 1,000 times to find the chance it won't occur at least once in ten centuries. The result, 37/100, indicates 63 chances in 100 that it will. In 10,000 years, by a similar calculation, there is only one chance in 20,000 that it could fail to happen. It is as near to a sure thing as you could ask for.

Aristotle once remarked that it was probable that the improbable would sometimes take place. Charlie Chan said: "Strange events permit themselves the luxury of occurring."

The calculus of chance can throw at least speculative light on human ancestry, too. Robert P. Stuckert, Ohio State University sociologist, has used it to estimate the degree of African ancestry in white Americans.

To construct a genetic probability table, Dr. Stuckert assumed the likelihood of mating between a person classified as white and one classified as Negro at one-twentieth of the random expectation. He used figures for natural increase and immigration; and from all these arrived at estimates for each census year.

For 1950 his tables indicate that of 135 million Americans listed as white, some 28 million had some African ancestry; and only about 4 million classified as Negroes were of pure African descent. He also estimated that in the previous ten years about 155,000 Negroes "passed" into the white category.

For those who call themselves white while maintaining that even a single remote African ancestor makes every descendant a Negro, there are some other interesting probability figures. Sixty generations ago the Roman Empire flourished; it knew no color bar; and people of varied color and origin moved through it. A man of European ancestry living today must calculate that he comes from 2^{60} ancestors of that Roman time, necessarily being related to many of them through many different lines, but surely taking in a great part of them all. That innocent little number, 2^{60}, works out to something more than a billion billion.

A new idea, which has been called a general theory of probability, links chance to relativity and, for that matter, space travel—where speeds approaching the velocity of light have been contemplated. As Einstein saw it, time would move more slowly as velocities increased. The hands of your space-ship wall clock would slow down and you would age only a few months—while those you left behind would age many years—on a near-maximum-speed trip to a near star and back.

The new theory, formulated by Dr. Nicholas Smith,

Jr., of Johns Hopkins, agrees. But the slowing, in Dr. Smith's view, would not be uniform. Your clock, and your biology, would slow down with "the jitters"—sometimes keeping time faster but more often slower, in a pattern following the laws of chance.

The workings of probability have interested writers in odd ways. In the manner of "for want of a nail," John Steinbeck, in *Cannery Row*, remarks the multiplications of chances by which one of the characters, sent hitch-hiking for an automobile part, failed to return:

"Oh, the infinity of possibility! How could it happen that the car that picked up Gay broke down before it got into Monterey? If Gay had not been a mechanic, he would not have fixed the car. If he had not fixed it the owner wouldn't have taken him to Jimmy Brucia's for a drink. And why was it Jimmy's birthday? Out of all the possibilities in the world—the millions of them—only events occurred that lead to the Salinas jail."

There is a short story, "The Law," by Robert M. Coates, that tells the disasters that follow when the law of averages breaks down.

The first hint of the breakdown comes when everybody in New York who owns an automobile decides to drive out to Long Island. This is not an instance of mass hypnotism, but merely a great, enormous, precedent-busting coincidence. The consequences are bedlam.

It is soon discovered that now theaters are jammed on some nights, practically empty on others. Lunchroom patrons have begun to make unpredictable runs on certain items, such as roast shoulder of veal with pan gravy.

In four days 274 successive customers in a notions store ask for a spool of pink thread.

One day—and again for no particular reason—the Twentieth Century Limited leaves for Chicago with just three passengers.

Congress finally has to act. After finding no evidence of Communist instigation, it notes that the Law of Averages has never been made statutory—and corrects the oversight.

From that day on, the law requires that people whose names begin with G, N, or U may go to theaters only on Tuesday, ball games only on Thursday, purchase clothing **only on** Mondays (between ten and noon). And so on into

many annoying, but now necessary, complications.

Again in literature, the ways of probability even wrest a moment of modesty from Conan Doyle's hero. After stringing a long series of guesses together to reconstruct the life of Dr. Watson's brother from looking at his watch, Sherlock Holmes is constrained to confess: "I could only say what was the balance of probability. I did not at all expect to be so accurate."

In *The Murders in the Rue Morgue*, Poe's brilliant detective Dupin says: "Coincidences, in general, are great stumbling-blocks in the way of that class of thinkers who have been educated to know nothing of the theory of probabilities—that theory to which the most glorious objects of human research are indebted for the most glorious of illustration."

Probability, which, then, means consistent behavior, is expected of the behavior of characters in fiction as it is of actual persons. Somerset Maugham has accused Dostoevsky of outraging the laws of probability in his treatment of Ivan in *The Brothers Karamazov*. Here, says Maugham, is a highly intelligent man, prudent, ambitious, and persistent. So his vacillation when hearing of the murder of his father is unaccountable. Dostoevsky failed to avoid the improbabilities—improbabilities of character, improbabilities of incident.

As John Gay put it:

> Lest men suspect your tale untrue,
> Keep probability in view.

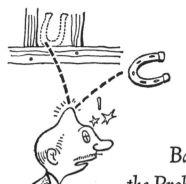

CHAPTER 11

How to Think About Luck

Baseball; bread and butter;
the Probable and the Wonderful;
the Surprise Index.

WHEN A baseball player comes to bat he may get on base and he may not, for reasons which are a mixture of skill and chance. If by the workings of these things 27 batters of a team fail in a row, a perfect no-hit game is produced. This has happened only three or four times in the 60,000-odd big-league games played in this century, each with two starting pitchers.

So experience says the odds against it are about 30,000 to 1, which is not out of line with a calculation of the probability. There may, of course, be other things to consider. What does the strain do to the pitcher as he realizes immortality is almost within reach? How does the umpire call a close pitch if his decision between ball and strike may make or break the potential no-hitter?

Even more remarkable than a no-hit game is what happened to a Cubs first-baseman. He played a full nine innings without once getting his hands on the ball, the only time this has happened in this century. If you figure that a first-baseman handles perhaps half the balls hit in a normal game, this occurrence works out to something that *should* happen only once in some hundreds of millions of games. On that basis, it probably will never happen again unless baseball proves a remarkably durable game.

Some amusing ways have been suggested for looking at pieces of luck like these.

Writing on "Probability, Rarity, Interest, and Surprise" in *The Scientific Monthly* (December 1948) Warren Weaver offers a way of figuring what he calls the Surprise Index. This S.I. is high when the improbable event is interesting. Any one bridge hand is exactly as improbable as any other, but most are not interesting enough to be surprising. A Yarborough, though not much use to anybody, is interestingly bad. It is much more interesting than it would be if it had not long ago been named and defined.

A "perfect hand" of 13 spades has a very high S.I. because we look at bridge hands in a certain way, putting everything that isn't perfect into one category and the 13-spader into another. So we are practically certain to get an imperfect hand, and a perfect hand is one chance in 635 billion.

Dr. Weaver concludes that a Surprise Index of 3 or 5 is not large, 10 begins to be surprising, 1,000 definitely is surprising, 1 million very surprising, "and 10^{12} would presumably qualify as a miracle."

In his book *The Dark Voyage and the Golden Mean* (Harvard University Press) Albert Cook says that there are two opposites in the pattern of living. They are the Wonderful and the Probable. We all yearn for the Wonderful, and the Probable is what most of us nearly always get.

When someone gets the Wonderful we call him lucky. When he gets the more favorable of even the fairly probable things repeatedly we may still call him lucky. That's a fair use of the word.

But we go wrong when we impute luck to him as something that he possesses, or when we give a predictive value to it. Gamblers and a lot of people who should know better do this, especially in circumstances such as gambling that are conducive to fuzzy thinking. A crap-shooter who makes several passes is likely to be judged to be in a hot streak, which is taken as reason to bet on him. In fact, though, the odds go right on being slightly against the shooter, as they always are in craps, and the profit continues to lie in betting he is "wrong."

The law of averages is the law of large numbers. Where chance is an important factor, conclusions based on a few instances remain highly untrustworthy—the fallacy of the small sample. A short trial of a business practice is likely to be inconclusive, one reason that theoretically sound enterprises often fail for lack of enough capital to ride out the run of bad breaks that is not at all unlikely to occur.

What, then, when a psychologist rules that you are extremely accident-prone if you have had many accidents, whether or not they were your fault? This denies that accidents are accidental, or it denies the laws of chance. Or possibly what it says is: Maybe your accidents were accidental but maybe not, and I'm not allowing you the benefit of the doubt. We don't want you working here.

Ethically this is on a par with giving a man an aptitude test of unknown validity and then firing him, or refusing to hire him, on the basis of the test result alone. But then, that's going on all the time.

In matters like these, and in a general sort of way, how

skeptical should we be? With so many ideas now discredited that the past held firmly, how can we be sure we know anything at all? The theory of probability gives us a useful way of answering this question: truth can never be attained, yet we can reach answers that are increasingly close to truth—that have a higher and higher degree of probability.

It helps to think of a line, marked 0 at one end and 1 at the other, with fractions such as .01, .25, .50, .75, .99 in between. The 0 end is for things we are sure are not true; the .01 represents the barest possibility, and so on to the 1, which stands for "absolutely true."

You may increase your intellectual responsibility if you stop to assign a place on such a line to an idea, an opinion, or a conviction . . . preferably before you assert it, act on it, or make it a fixed part of your mental equipment. This is the philosophical equivalent of the mathematical expectation touched on in connection with insurance and gambling in Chapter 2.

At least a mild skepticism is in order when the probabilities appear to be flouted. A coin may turn up heads a dozen times in a row, and in any long run it is almost certain to do so occasionally, but it doesn't hurt to stop for a glance at the other side. You can be short-changed by honest error, but you are entitled to wonder what's going on if there never seems to be a mistake in your favor.

In this connection there is a story of a father, a man of observant and speculative turn. He was interested to note that when his children dropped their bread it invariably landed butter-side up.

"This," he said, "is in utter defiance of the laws of chance."

After ten of these happy accidents in a row, against odds of something better than a thousand to one, he investigated.

The kids, he discovered, were buttering their bread on both sides.

CHAPTER 12

Probability Problems and Puzzles

I. The Coinciding Birthday Parties

You have, let's say, 24 friends who give parties on their birthdays. You can attend only one party on any day. What would you guess the chances to be that you'll have to miss a party because more than one falls on the same day of the year?

This is a fine instance of the difficulty of judging complex probabilities by common sense. It is actually somewhat more likely than not that you'll have to pass up a party.

Figure it this way. The first birthday can be any day. There is one chance in 365 that the second will come on the same day—or 364 in 365 that it will not. That the third will coincide with either of the first two is two chances in 365—or 363 in 365 that it will not. So multiply 364/365 by 363/365 and so on to 342/365. It comes out .46, or slightly less than an even chance that the birthdays won't coincide.

For 26 birthdays, which comes to one every other week of the year, it's .37 or almost 2 to 1 odds that at least two birthdays will fall on the same day.

Even-money bets on this would be highly profitable in the long run, or even the fairly short run, and shouldn't be hard to get, since the conclusion we've proved rather outrages common sense. You might agree to settle the bet by opening "Who's Who" at random and taking the first 26 birth dates given.

II. The Teen-Age Brides

A magazine writer argues the danger of youthful marriage with census figures showing that "the percentage of separations due to marital difficulties of teen-age married women (4.0 to 4.4 in ages 14 to 19) was a full point higher than in any other age group."

Why doesn't this prove anything against the kids?

Did you catch the weakness in the argument?

The difference, for all you can tell, may be entirely due to the fact that all the wedded teen-agers are in the first, most difficult, years of marriage. All other age groups are bound to include many who have been married longer.

To get a real comparison of probabilities, you'd better set the teen-agers' records against those of older brides in the *same years* of marriage.

III. The Dangerous Jumps

In the Pierre Boule novel The Bridge *over the River Kwai there's a nice exercise in probability. Three Commandos are to be parachuted into the Siamese jungle for sabotage against Japanese forces. An RAF officer has been asked if, in default of the regular course, for which there is not enough time, he can give them some quick training. He advises against it in these words:*

". . . if they do only one jump, you know, there's a fifty per cent chance of an injury. Two jumps, it's eighty per cent. The third time, it's dead certain they won't get off scot free. You see? It's not a question of training, but the law of averages."

What's wrong with the calculation?

If the chance of coming safely to earth is 1/2 for one jump, it must be $1/2 \times 1/2$ for two, $1/2 \times 1/2 \times 1/2$ for three. Subtract these products from 1 and you find the probabilities of injuries on two or three jumps actually are 75% and 87½%.

In the story, incidentally, all three go in and none is hurt—a rather good piece of luck against odds of 7 to 1. If you accept the officer's reasoning you'll have to rate this a miracle.

IV. The Simple Midshipman

Captain Marryat, in "Peter Simple," tells of the midshipman who prudently put his head through a hole made in the side of his ship by an enemy ball and kept it there through the rest of the battle. Said he: "By a calculation made by Professor Inman, the odds are 32,647 and some decimals to boot, that another ball will not come in at the same hole."

The tale's amusing, but the fallacy is a basic one, responsible for many wrong conclusions.

Many soldiers in World War I shared this notion and favored fresh shell holes for shelter, arguing it was highly unlikely that two shells would hit any one given spot in the same day. True—but once the spot has been hit it is just as likely as any other spot to take the next shell.

V. How to Win a Coin Toss

A book on betting and chance offers, in all seriousness, this strategy for winning on a coin toss. Let the other man make the call, for if you are the one who calls, the chances are 3 to 2 against you. Explanation: 7 out of 10 people will cry heads, but heads will turn up only 5 times out of 10, so if you let your opponent call, you have the greater probability of winning.

This is a bit of nonsense of the same order as "heads I win, tails you lose." But it does sound convincing, doesn't it? Of course it doesn't make a bit of difference who makes the call or what it is; the chances remain fifty-fifty every time.

VI. What Magazine D'ya Read?

The same author investigated your chances of reading Life *magazine. They're pretty bad, he says, unless you make $2,500 a year (this was some time ago) "because that is the average earning power of a* Life *reader."*
   How about it?

Doesn't mean a thing, unless you know a little about the deviation from the mean. The average income of people who breathe may be $2,500 too, but that doesn't mean that breath-drawers are scarcer in one income group than in another.

VII. The Three-Card Flush

Now let's get to something practical. What are the chances of drawing successfully to a three-card flush?
   (Interpretation, mainly for non-players: Having been dealt three spades and two non-spades from a deck of 52, you throw away the useless two and draw two more cards from the deck. How likely is it both will be spades?)

Of the 47 cards you don't know about, 10 are spades, giving you a probability of 10/47 that your first draw will be a spade. If it is, you will then have 9 chances in 46 of getting another one. Multiply the two fractions together and what you get will reduce to about 1/24.

So drawing to a three-card flush is bucking odds of 23 to 1. Try it rarely if ever.

VIII. The Well-Dressed Pedestrian

This squib is from the magazine California Highways: *"A large metropolitan police department made a check of the clothing worn by pedestrians killed in traffic at night. About four-fifths of the victims were wearing dark clothes and one-fifth light-colored garments. This study points up the rule that pedestrians are less likely to encounter traffic mishaps at night if they wear or carry something white after dark so that drivers can see them more easily."*

Well, what does this really point up?

It emphasizes the principle that white sheep eat more than black sheep. There are more of them.

This evidence is worthless. For all we know, at least four-fifths of the people who walk along dark highways wear dark clothes, which is certainly the way it seems to a driver. If so, no wonder more reach the morgue. Again, there are more of them.

IX. The Combination Lock

If the combination of a lock is RED, or some other group of three letters, how many possible combinations might be used?

There are 26 possibilities for each of the three letters—26³ or 17,576. This is why the state of California switched from all-number vehicle license plates to ones using three letters followed by numbers. (There are only a thousand ways to combine three numbers.) Of course, quite a few of the added combinations were lost by the time a staff of linguists weeded out anything that might be offensive in any language.

If repetition is not allowed, three letters may be combined in only $26 \times 25 \times 24$ ways, or 15,600.

X. The Tricky Dice

This one is meaner than it looks. What is the chance of throwing at least one ace when you toss a pair of dice?

These "at least" problems are best tackled backwards. The chance of *not* throwing an ace with each of the dice is 5/6. Since $5/6 \times 5/6$ is 25/36, there are 11 chances in 36 (1 minus 25/36) of throwing at least one ace.

XI. The Rare Dollar Bill

The Arthur Murray people broadcast an offer of $25 worth of dancing lessons to anyone who could find in his wallet a dollar bill of which the serial number contains any of the digits 2, 5, or 7.

There are eight digits in such a serial number. What's the chance that a bill chosen at random would win the prize?

Excellent. For each digit, the chance that it will not be one of the mystic numbers is 7/10. The product of this fraction taken eight times is about .058, or 1/18. Seventeen dollar bills out of every 18 will qualify.

Does this hint that Arthur Murray wants everybody to win a prize? It does indeed, particularly when you note that the same sponsor makes a similar offer to anyone who can identify such broadcast "mystery" tunes as "Jingle Bells."

At another time Murray offered his prize in return for a "Lucky Buck" containing both a 5 and a 0. How rare an item would this be? I leave that one for you to play with.

XII. The Three-Card Game

A sharp operator shows you three cards. One is white on both sides. One is red on both sides. The other is white on one side and red on the other. He mixes the cards in a hat, lets you take one without looking and place it flat on the table.

The upper side turns out to be white. "It's obvious," says the sharper, "that this is not the red-red card. It must be one of the other two, so the reverse side can be either red or white. Even so, I'll be generous. I'll bet you a dollar against seventy-five cents that the other side is also white."

Is this a fair bet? Or does it actually favor you, as it appears to?

Neither. It's a sure long-run money-maker for your sharp friend.

The trick is that there are not two possible cases but three, and the three are equally probable.

In one case the other side is red. In both other cases it is white, since it may be either side of the white-white card.

The odds thus are 2 to 1 that the other side is white, and the sharp fellow will win seventy-five cents from you twice for each once that he loses a dollar.

This is a particularly difficult thing to understand, or at least to believe. If you are not convinced, make a good run of trials and see how it works out.

XIII. The Tricky Air Force

A lieutenant writes me that the Air Force hornswoggled him when he was an ROTC senior, using statistics that "proved" jet flying safer than flying in conventional craft. Their gist: the death rate, in fatalities per 100,000 aircraft hours, is higher in ordinary planes than in jets.

What gimmick did the lieutenant spot a little late?

The catch, as the officer says he began to realize after reading a book called *How to Lie with Statistics,** is in the number of people aboard. Fighting jets carry crews of one or two, other planes five to ten or more. Many more people are exposed to risk per aircraft hour in a conventional plane because it is bigger, but that does not mean the danger is as great or greater for any individual.

This kind of propaganda is equivalent to advising you

* It has funny pictures, too.

to move from New York or California to Nevada for your health. After all, fewer people died in Nevada last year.

If genuine information had been the aim, the figures might better have been for deaths per million man-hours or man-miles. Choice between these last two is a splendid subject for argument.

XIV. The 10-Man Free-for-All

Watch out for this one. It's double-barreled.

Ten men enter a game of chance, such as coin-flipping. Each has the same capital, five pennies or whatever you like. The rules say the first two, selected by lot, will play till one wins all the other's money. Then he will take on another player to the death, and so on. Eventually the survivor of the first nine will play against the last man.

Now the question: who has the best chance to win— one of the first pair of players, the last player to enter, or some one of the others?

The first part of this double question involves the effect of amount of capital on a player's chances in any contest. The answer to this has some helpful applications, which you might care to ponder, on playing the stock market, starting a business, or bucking a roulette wheel.

The rule is that a contestant's chances of eventual victory are in exact proportion to his stake. The mathematical proof is complicated, but the logic is apparent. If you are to risk twice as much as your opponent, you should have twice his chance of winning. Thus your expectation (the amount you stand to win multiplied by your probability of winning it) will be equal to his, a requirement of a fair game.

All right. Each of the first players has a probability of winning the first round of 1/2. The winner then has twice the capital of his next opponent, giving him a probability of 2/3 to 1/3 of victory. The winner this time will enter the next round with his own stake plus that of two losers. His chance to win then is 3/4.

Follow this logic through and you will find that the chance of eventual victory for one of the first pair of contestants is $1/2 \times 2/3 \times 3/4 \times 4/5$ and so on to 9/10. Since each numerator cancels the preceding denominator, you will discover in a matter of seconds that this product is 1/10.

The player who begins with the second round does so with only half his opponent's capital. His chance of going into the third round is thus only 1/3, but after that the sequence is the same as just figured—$1/3 \times 3/4 \times 4/5$ and so on. His chance also works out to 1/10.

In the same way you can demonstrate the same probability for each of the other players in turn. The last player to enter will do so with only one coin for each nine his opponent has accumulated. The odds are 9 to 1 against him, and his probability of winning is 1 in 10.

So oddly enough it makes no difference in which round of the free-for-all you enter the contest.

XV. The Maturity of the Chances

You are engaged in flipping a nickel one hundred times. By a rare but possible chance, you get heads on all the first twenty tosses. A friend points out that since the law of averages says you should get about 50 heads in any hundred trials, you can expect only 30 heads to 50 tails in the rest of your series.

That's right, isn't it?

Of course you didn't fall for this ancient fallacy. As you explained to your misguided friend, a nickel has no memory. It will tend to produce 50% heads from now on without regard to what it happened to do in the past. After 20 heads, the expectation for the total run is now about 60 heads to 40 tails.

XVI. The Triangle of Pascal

In a family of 10 children, what is the likelihood that 3 will be girls and 7 will be boys?

Or, not counting the 0, what is the probability that red will come up 3 times in 10 plays at roulette?

Or that you will get heads exactly 3 times in 10 flips of a penny?

You can find the answer, which of course is the same for all three questions, by tediously listing all the 1,024 possible arrangements and counting up the number that meet the specification. This will take a great deal of patience.

Or you can work out the coefficients of a binomial expansion, in this case $(x + y)^{10}$. Having worked out the problem of $x + y$ times itself 9 times, you'll get a result that starts like this and goes on for quite a while:

$$x^{10} + 10x^9y + 45x^8y^2 + 120x^7y^3 \ldots$$

The coefficients are the numbers in front of the terms, including the 1 which is understood to be in front of the first term. They will add up to 1,024. The probability that all of 10 children will be boys is the coefficient of the first term, or 1 (in 1,024). The second coefficient gives you the chances of 9 boys to 1 girl, 10 (in 1,024). The third gives it for 8 boys to 2 girls (45), and the fourth tells you that the answer to our question is 120 chances in 1,024, or about 2 in 17.

If that sounds laborious (and it is), you may like an ancient system for arriving at the same result. You can create what is known as the triangle of Pascal very easily from memory any time you want to solve this kind of problem.

Write down two 1's side by side. This gives the possible results of one toss of a coin: one chance of heads, one of tails, adding up to the total number of possibilities, which is 2.

Below and to the left and below and to the right, put two more 1's. There will be a gap between them. Fill it with the sum of the two numbers most nearly above this gap. Since they are 1's, write 2.

Put 1's at the extremes of the third line also. Fill the two gaps with 3's, since the numbers above the gaps are 2 and 1.

When you finish the tenth line—and you can go on indefinitely—you'll have the triangle you see below.

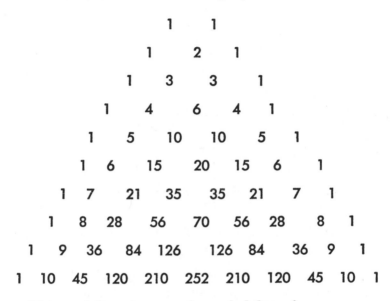

This tenth line gives you the probabilities for a sequence of 10 children, or 10 coin-tosses, or any other series of 10 even chances. The total of all the numbers across is 1,024. So the number at the left, 1, gives the chance in 1,024 that all will be girls, if that's what we're talking about. The 10 is for the chance of a 9-to-1 proportion in the specified direction, and so on to the big number in the middle. This, as you might expect, tells you that there are 252 chances in 1,024 of a fifty-fifty mix.

It's useful to note that although this even break is by far the most likely single probability, the odds are quite strongly against it as compared with the total of the others. It is in fact less likely than a 6-4 assortment (210 + 210 = 420 chances in 1,024) if you allow this to be either 6 girls and 4 boys or the other way about.

And that is true of many of the things that the laws of probability show. Even the most probable of a set of possibilities may be quite improbable.